I0821664

The Gamekeeper

The Gamekeeper

SELECTED POEMS 1976–2011

MICHAEL HARRIS

The Porcupine's Quill

Library and Archives Canada Cataloguing in Publication

Harris, Michael, 1944–
[Poems. Selections]
The gamekeeper : selected poems, 1976–2011 / Michael Harris.

ISBN 978-0-88984-407-0 (softcover)

I. Title.

PS8515.A7894A6 2017 C811'.54 C2017-905096-6

1 2 3 • 19 18 17

Published by The Porcupine's Quill, 68 Main Street, PO Box 160, Erin, Ontario N0B 1T0. http://porcupinesquill.ca

Readied for the press by Carmine Starnino.

Represented in Canada by Canadian Manda.
Trade orders are available from University of Toronto Press.

We acknowledge the support of the Ontario Arts Council and the Canada Council for the Arts for our publishing program. The financial support of the Government of Canada is also gratefully acknowledged.

Clarior Hinc Honos

Table of Contents

Sparks (1976)

Grace (1977)

In Transit (1985)

New and Selected Poems (1992)

Circus (2011)

Sparks

(1976)

The Human Element

Steadily, as fine water fretting,
drip by drip, lines on rock,
Audrey dug the garden; the Lebruns
before her, and before them the Neilsons,

who let the nail fall
that punctured her heel, the blood running
in me quickly and nothing I could do then
not to have it happen.

On that day apple blossoms fell;
there were falling stars and the moon
had the shadow of the earth move fully across it.
I had been netting butterflies, unable to sit

under the apple and feel the tree was home,
unable to pierce what I wasn't seeing with a poem.

Birthday in Late November

Thin as water
in a winter stream,
the radio runs down.

Two days of snow:
each day a half-foot
and tomorrow, more snow.

The house is as stone
under the snow: so the crow
might see it. More kindly, I find it

bone in a bleach
of white sand, bone-strong
and indicating life.

A patchwork of frost coats the window;
it is unspeakably
full of flowers.

There is a silence that contains
even the crow; all the other animals
are under the cover of snow.

A horizon of fields spreads out beyond my fences;
they are sponge-clean and perfectly
without tracks. I am here at the end

of a closed road,
with time to learn
many kinds of laughter.

To begin, I go
to the window, seeking
evidences for and against me.

The Patient

I am here and afraid; my body
scooped out and laid in thin
rubber, the tubes like thermometers
in my body's weather; they fill me

with bread pale as clean cotton.
I reduce it, reduce everything
to liquids in what's left of my stomach,
in what's left of my mind.

In the softest, quietest ways I am broken
into parts; one a day, once a day, they
come and play with me, with red sacs
and white sacs and murmurings and measurements.

They clean me like a fingernail
where the quick starts to sting
and they will not stop.

A Woman Washing Clothes Sees a Heron

Blue mark on the skin of blue water,
the heron moves for silver prey in silence.
Methodically she combs the random reeds
and near the shore she hesitates:
the sun's a deep-red egg nested on an edge
of blue gauze as quick, twitch, flip-of-the-wrist
the day is slowly-shaking silk straightening out.

At noon the woman tends to laundry on the line,
mending sky with sheets and the fuss of shirts.
Skinny fists gripped in a string of washing,
fishing for stillness, she watches the bird,
dumb to an intricacy a flight beyond her fancy.
The claw strikes, stalks, strikes and her blood
is a vehicle for fear; all her body seems unmuscled.

Things get eaten. The sky shifts colour.
Turning past the line of light the sun goes down
and goes down. She dreams a white crane alone
and risen from a field which is blue; and herself
beating stone-ground wheat, bony hands brown
with sun pounding dun grain-dough in a gourd-drum:
an image only, something to trespass into
the corner of an eye.
 And her hand, then, the heronfist
on the straw edge of the heronnest, and the sun gone
red again, dribbled over the lip of the world.
And her fist undone thinking What is this, this
red fish squirming like a heart in my body,
a line of white sheets shapeless on the ground?

The Sparks

A wooden chair, a table, a few
remaining books and a bowl

my girl made me, these I saw
when the wind blew down through the chimney

and the fire billowed out at the room.
Some would think it poverty to live

surrounded by so few things,
or simple the heat the fire gives.

The fire arights itself, shouldering
its smoke skywards; the sparks

fade like old stars on the carpet,
leaving the smallest of scars.

Grace

(1977)

The Gamekeeper

The salmon is still
in the noiseless black; she was quick-silvered
star to the ship whose hull
has sunk below the bottom of the lake.
The weeds stand stiff
in the shivering dark, and the gamekeeper's gone

whose bears are now shadows
long done with their powers
in the mud-and-cold land.
The vixen's neat paws print
the news in black stars
but the secret's gone quick
and dug deeper. Autumn's hold
has been broken
a million times over
and it's snowing.

The bright hummingbirds flew
to find their hearts in
a frenzy, for the sky was a flower
that had lost its centre
and the swarms in the air
were snow. Now they know all there is to know
of dark. And the gamekeeper's gone

whose crow's a tattoo
at the top of a tree, losing his grip
at the too-thin tip
of the cold that is pricking him bare.
He thinks war
and it's war though the summer's surrendered
and raised its white flag
a million times over
and it's snowing.

Now the waddling porcupine's swaying his quills
all at sea in the swaddle
of his winter fat;
he is slow in the sudden
and no match at all
for the silk and soft skins
of winter. He chews bark,
for the gamekeeper's gone

whose snakes took green with them
and wove it in a bundle
and buried it under a rock,
for the earth had stopped in tatters
and lay down dead-white
dead-skinned, belly-up
and not right. Then the wind coiled hugely,
struck and coiled and shed its white
a million times over
and it's snowing.

Plump rats and grey weasels channel blindly
their fright, clawing squealing
at their tunnels: to core them, seal them, escape
from the light, from the ache
of a world wide with snow; but their black brains
are caught, are furnaced with the spark:
the gamekeeper's gone

whose starving, still hopeful, pure panic of deer
tiptoe the brittle-twigged landscape to silence
to a deadhalt
at the appletree; and the appletree's victory stays
stiff-necked, full of thrash
in its iron-bare head of black antler,
in the slow-moving barrens of its branches
where the sky falls to pieces

sinking deeper and deeper
a million times over;

and it's snowing on the otter
whose eye is a film of ice.
It whispers blessing the shivering field-mouse
whose heaven is black with snow.
It is snowing on the hare
whose fur is a layer of winter.
It falls against the houses,
against the drinkers in the bars,
a million times over. The gamekeeper's gone.

The fields harden fast
around their stone.

October at the Farm

The last apples in the garden are down
 or hang frozen in the grey air.
The apple-dump slithers under the rubber feet

of rats whose eyes are the black-bulbed ends
 of steel pins driving hunger through their brains.
The cold is a trap that is sure of its aim.

Though I close my own eyes, there is no exit.
 Though I draw the strings impossibly tight
around the sacks, seal the canning-jars, still October's

sweet rot ciders the air. The neat lawn shivers
 against the silvering licks of wind
and fights back to green; but it's toothless and soft

and can't hold. Here, in the harrowed, cut-open earth
 the rats worm like leeches at a wound.
They follow in the dark their pink mouths

with a smell like soured milk on a baby's breath.

The Woods

I know the mole's slow heart
troubles still with the mole's dull blood

and her glass eyes have filled
with dark. She lies made of mud

at the end of her burrowing,
still as sediment, a sludge.

The cells in the trees themselves are slow
as molecules in iron; they have almost lost

their life, the one great heart-beat
giving green in spring. In a wind come cold

from the ends of the earth, a dog-fox waits
for blood, for some sign, an eye;

he is watcher to a world that holds
his breath. Somewhere near is the rabbit's fur

harrowed white with the quiet fears
of winter. Nothing changes here.

My skis-and-poles cut and stitch neatly
the unkillable body of the world; I make

my human passage through this wood, watching
each track vanish in the brilliances of snow

with the bloods and torn hides of animals.
At each sudden crack of the frozen branches

my own hide hackles with terror; yet something
else gains its peace with each easy glide

of the skis, with the sky-high howl of the hungry
and the silence of the prey.

Barn Swallow

Metal-still on the shed-roof tin
 until it cocks its head
to eye the world
 which has begun to crack
its own black shell

 until its claws pull
its body in
with soft trigger-pressures it's up
 and up higher
all up in an arc wheeling down swooping
and screaming smoothly down dead
 on the twisting trail
 of a dragonfly which turns
quickly in the silver
 signals of its wings
until the swallow takes that silver
 for treasure in its beak
and the beak's blunt scissor
 shuts down hard
and harder then the bird pitches down
 the sheer cliffs of air
slipstreaming God
 to the shed-roof where it sits
and eats

and is
out again spinning
a thin blade turning
on a dotty moth dazed from every side by light
 and stoneblinded surely by
 this cataract of black

and is an air-ace barnstorming
 stealing the stomachs of the watchers

with its dolphin's bounce from an air to an air
and twists tricks turnings for the joy of it

and flies butterfly-fluttery
at all the edges of the sky

and there turns as quickly
as a liar in a lie

The Ice Castle

Even now, mid-winter,
something light, alive,
is shining from the depths of it.

When I touch its perfect skin,
the light shimmers melting
in small streams of water.

How delicate the dream
that even ice
attempts to hold.

Art

I want to be the man
　　　in Rodin's *The Kiss*
or Brancusi's *The Kiss*

I want to be among
　　　the essential
kissers of all time

I know a kiss
　　　is just a kiss
is just a cushioned push

of face, a slippery wash
　　　of lips that blush
then turn to ice, to fall

lake-ice, to ice as
　　　delicate as lace
as hard and cold as love

whose dream is seed
　　　and blood red and not
these soft kisses, breathless

Shadfly

If it keeps
to its legs

in this spindly light,
this amber cathedral this nothingness,

it will be a miracle.
Not a step but it stops

and bends hesitantly closer.
Now it leans

its head down, is a man
at his prayer

to not let
that nothingness

catch him.

Frogs Courting

is hardsell, a noise
that raises every minute

the pitch of patience
into a new key.

April's heat slowcooks this seethe;
and stretches and thins, refines the din

until the dark itself
aches with it.

What stops them
is applause: a clap.

They think it's
the end of the world; or maybe

the marriage-proposal's starting-gun.
Or maybe quietly they're bowing at

this compliment to their techniques.
Whatever they think, they keep up that singing:

it's the party spring gives
all over the country-blocks;

and the folk for whom it's given
are the tadpoles and the hawks.

The Lepidopterist's Letter

Now even the moths are quiet.
Twelve miles away, a month ago, someone saw
that green one. He didn't get it either.

September is a thirty-day month: forever
I like to think. It makes me feel better.
I sat for a time in the bake of the porch

training my eyes to undo their camouflage;
in an hour I would ache. The entire landscape
became a mirage. Then blinded at night

by the swirl around the shed-light, I tired
of searching for the Luna. Its Latin name
is *actias luna*. What remains now is the nest

you admired: of wasps, by the way, not bees.
It is larger now, and light grey; I think they
have finished building it. It looks like stone

made of paper. The slightest wind explodes it.
In the evenings it catches light
from the bloated harvest-moon.

It hangs from the rafters like a heart.

Uncle Edward

Had the earth one more than four corners ...
Had fire more life than good drink ...
If the air did more than just *be* there!

But Uncle Edward's pink is tickled fully by water:
hot baths, the certainties of porcelain, the mists
which keep his basso like a wealth

of large slow fish swimming at idle
in the steamy air. He loves even the golden rain
of urine boiling its froth in the toiletbowl.

In his baths, each plip-ploop from the silver taps
is pitch-note for a whiskied hymn to women,
to water, to whisky, whatever! Each drip moves,

like a fishing-bob, the winking pink of his penis.
Outlandishly it peeks from the bulk of him
at the love-songs and war-songs that wheel

circling each other above him; it eyes with awe
the patient polysyllables he herds like pods of whales
for a final sally through the Valley of the Shadow.

Later, in bed, in a dry shroud of sheets,
he dreams a death at sea, watching his voice
rise up in bubbles past a parterre

of ungrateful urchins and bored whelks, past
a mezzanine's yawn of oysters, past a loge
stuffed with an awestruck, round-eyed gawk

of groupers, up through the roof of the sea,
past an exhausted mating codfish eaten whole
by a hungry shark; and with the bubbles expanding hugely

sail directly up to Heaven past the sun's
dying fire, past the thinning insufficiencies
of air, beyond the earth's wasting corpse

to burst in liquid glories, drowning
Heaven's whole angelic chorus with
the mortal heart and humour of his song.

Deacon Moth

The light's banged
its bell: the spider's pulled back
like a fist in his corner.

The Deacon's at the wall, skittish
as a feather-duster. Slow as a rag-picker,
panic takes the colour from his wings.

Still the spider sticks
to its corner, heedless of the flurry,
the motoring worry of worn-thin wings.

Here, he says, Look: I have nothing
up my sleeves. And moves his magician's cloth
closer. But the Deacon discovers

that light itself is trembling, and
it flutters and tugs, and the whole
world is ending where it

hung from a thread.

Rabbit

The white rabbit died
in a twist of fur; and death

dulled its eyes that were
moon-iced yet.

Now it hangs on a hook
on a beam in the kitchen,

dull-eyed, scarlet-mouthed,
still-whiskered; still

leaping
from the hook

with its legs
bound tight.

The Hunting-Cabin in November

Not a soul about
but the spinsterish
birches. They have strayed

from the woods, clinging vaguely
in clumps thin as curls
round an old woman's neck.

They gather in whispers by the ones
that have cracked their backs,
broken their bodies at the knees.

The tired ones lean
their heads toward the ground
and their skins peel off

like paper. In these woods there are
no souls about but clumps
of dry sticks with the raspberries gone,

with their frail shoots frozen,
gripping stiffly at the air
like the skeletal legs

of dead spiders. The twelve-gauge glistens
with bluing and rests frozen on its rack.
The white-tail keeps her blood warm in the woods.

Death & Miss Emily

DEATH

watches Miss Emily
at dawn; she is dressing

at her vanity, all in white,
without fuss, but underwater-floating,

half-groggily submerged
in a lulling pool of sleepiness.

Weathered billets-doux hang pinned
in the sheen of black crepe

that encloses her looking-glass
like a wreath of wet seaweed.

Her face rests slightly wavering
in the muddy depths of the mirror:

a flat flounder momentarily at idle.
As through water the sunlight

weakly soaks its glow on the cotton curtains.
Death peers into his quiet aquarium.

DEATH

sets fat slugs
at the glisten of the apple-dump.

They begin their inch, sticking to the tips
of the apple-leaves like fat, black pearls.

In the thicket by the Looking-Pool's still, jade depth
a large vixen trembles exhausted

giving her cubs good suck
on the underbelly bloods of a rabbit.

Nightcrawlers concertina back into the black
of their holes with a small sound.

The morning sun pours its hard light
as through a diamond's chill heart.

Death has everything
groomed to receive her.

MISS EMILY

feels a doubt crawl her skin.

Immediately Death adopts her face
and peers closely from the mirror

at this doubt, at every blemish,
at all the scars and delicate veins

that root his joy. Against the white of the room,
the window gains its crimson, like a rose.

The doubt struggles carefully
like an eel in thick weeds

and brushes the hairs of shiver
that stiffen on the nude neck of Miss Emily.

She closes firmly the buttons of her frock.
She counts the hard strokes of her hairbrush.

MISS EMILY

stands from the mirror and the world
falls into place about her.

She cleans her room. She attends to the sprawl
of her boots, seals the tongues, sews shut

the gape of eyes with tight lace.
She sees nothing now but neatness.

As she descends
the room rises

brightly from its use
like the sun's slow soar

from its ashes. Death watches
the falling minutes start

their relentlessly monotonous dissolve
of light.

Miss Emily feels the radiance
of sunlight rise in her

like an alcohol warmed in a flame.
She is drunk. She is giddy as a fish

swirled slowly in the first soft reaches of a maelstrom.
She reels with her giddiness as into a lake

which holds her and rolls her and drowns her
with delight until her laughter ripens

like bubbles and her small chest tightens
and wants air, air, air, stopping sober

at the surface

the third time up.

MISS EMILY

hears the village's big parson
at matins. She feels his sweat,

she sees his big fist blacken,
pounding the cover of his Bible raw.

She knows how his imagination conjures angels and hellfires
and the horrible contortions of the damned;

how his mouth labours athletically, at grace,
at the effort of catching up

to his hairtrigger, grapeshot mind.
Calmly Miss Emily cleans, humming a hymn

while Death sets aflame small candles of grass
with dew and with sunlight.

He listens with care at the latticed confessional
of the kitchen window. Miss Emily eats honey

and hums, hearing the bees drone by
trawling for honey, blessing each bowed head

in the parish of clover, keeping
their poisons to themselves.

She watches the bees on their full flat
of summer lilies: simple syllables of noise,

the earth taking wing like a language on a tongue.
What Death hears is the settling of the wax

at the cells of the honey-hive. He sees drones die.
He approves whole-heartedly the stone look of the hive.

He admires the idea of all of that sweetness
plugged-up paper-thin in its womb.

MISS EMILY

is pulling at the strain
of the morning visit like a kite.

She takes root
and holds there, at the top of the stairs,

her powerdam of joy, her tinderbox despair,
her stored voltages of speech.

Her words, bits of wit
skitter into the gloom

of the hat-racks and cape-hooks
on short fuses.

She wants men, their power
glossed stiffly in serge, with a patina

as soft as satin. She loves the mysteries
of flesh, of flesh moving

in dark suits, in the dark
fashion of the times.

But there is nowhere the man to court her
and nowhere the man to wed.

The men in the vestibule shuffle
as underneath a weight,

their powers flagging sadly
like a Basset-hound's loose, glum face.

With a stutter of apology, stemming from some
possible disagreement, a visitor has spoken

loudly. With great poise, and much unsaid,
Miss Emily goes quietly to her room,

excusing herself
with a little smile.

DEATH

has Miss Emily's two other suitors in his pocket:
one in the pulpit and the other on the bench.

They prayed for her at first, extending
a hand, bending a knee; at the last they

courted her judiciously, with all the right
words. But when Miss Emily's heart

bursts with joy light birds
and terror and blood, when she cries and shouts

offers and thinks and writes and writes
love love love love love love love,

they go, quietly, shattered, back to their posts.
Death understands instantly

that his best institutions are institutions—
and multiplies them immediately; then appoints

one drop of his own precious blood
to hold court in Miss Emily's heart.

hears her bobolink, her high-flier
come circling over

the Puritan face of her village.
She listens to its gossip

of worms and babies, an adoration
of everything alive and dead,

like the dance of sunlight
glittering on the silver rims

of the spectacles of soldiers
with half their skulls shot away.

She cleans to a simple sparkle
the glass of the library windows with

the crumpled pages of the news of the day, singing
bob o'lincoln, bob lincoln, bobolink.

And she listens to the ocean
in the sea-shell of her heart.

She hears blood: it is wind settling
in the leaves with a whisper. It is water

pounding the Atlantic to nothing, to sand
at the edge of the sea. It is the running, red

foam of wheatfields at sundown. It laughs energetically
in wars, in storms. Its life is the vein

of vacuum at the core of cyclones. She marvels
at the fathoms of green in the meadows

but understands the lava writhing
seething slow-dragonish underneath.

Intensely she listens to the bird,
to her heart. She hears blood.

She hears Death, Death.
She hears Death.

MISS EMILY

winds the mantel-clock at mid-day,
her face in its face. She is trapped.

She is bare as the world in the infinite
fall into space, but smaller, and barer,

a fish scooped into the steel-cold slops
of a ship, scalded in salt-air, turned belly-up,

the hopeless softnesses bared in the hard sunlight
as for intimate inspections. The clock releases

twelve golden notes through its silvery rattle
of chain. She stands absolutely still.

She is trapped. She scrambles upward drowning
breathless not moving all uphill like a fish

swimming its infinity of mile in a glass tank.
She stops winding, stands absolutely still.

DEATH

arranges the blueberries, just before tea,
in a rich galaxy of green, high on the hillside,

like mute, dull planets.
Miss Emily sees them differently: she pretends

they are the shadowed eyes of children
in an orphanage: the same eyes every year,

but with new faces. Or they are the beads
of a broken rosary

which endlessly she must gather
to gain an access to God.

She has no children. Is there a God?
Miss Emily holds her basket of blueberries.

She scans the sky for clues: cloud
but no voice. She examines the Looking-Pool:

all water, all reflection, without beginning,
without end. She searches the hillside: nothing

but her shadow frailly holding
its watery lengthening brand

and, deeper in the green, the dusty-dull
millions of blueberries.

MISS EMILY

loves apples. A green apple
is Faith, with its bitter reward.

Red apples are Hope. They are eaten
when ripest. Gold apples are Charity

until they drop into the rot of the apple-dump.
Of the three she chooses Charity; she picks off

the slugs and pulls out the worms
which appals Death, who has taken great trouble

to set it all up. He feels rejected.
He has Miss Emily go over to the raspberries.

She sees a battlefield of green shoots and brittle canes,
the canes brown as bone, with air for marrow.

She picks off one red, soft thimble,
baring the delicate, skeletal end.

She sees her own fingers stained red.
Gently she touches the bared, soft nub.

DEATH

engineers the blackberries'
apostasy through the falling-apart

of the silken white petals, the hairy
jade-green of the first spring buttons,

the gathering ambers warming mid-summer,
the August wine-red distilling its ruby,

keeping black through the spectrum undamaged.
Then he bulbs them black-purple and liquid as the eyes

of victorious generals; and hones the thorn
bone-hard as a hawk's hooked beak.

Miss Emily picks them with care, grinds them
to grit and pulps them for juices

and boils them in a cauldron, strains them in bags
and strings them up dripping deep purple

and stacks the used bags like spent Union soldiers
and colours the labels Confederate grey.

But Death sets the wild strawberries trembling
like sweet girls' hearts

that would burst in the air and shrivel and dry
if not taken. But the berries run their bloods

in Miss Emily's white porcelains
all properly public, like sheets after weddings.

She sugars their sweetness, cloys them
in syrups, boils them and clots them and joins them

with rhubarbs, stiffens them
with apples and marries them

to blackness
in a row of glass jars.

DEATH

watches Miss Emily
take tea, while he

takes pleasure in attending
Miss Emily's neighbour's garden party.

He borrows the musician, whose heart is weak.
From the finger-slim plectrums of a spinet

come sprinklings of Christmas hymns
with the anaesthetic quietude of snow;

and then the springy jarring leaps,
the recklessly escaping bursts, of summer;

then the after-music silence
through which the stream still moves

to the Looking-Pool and the planets
keep their course. A sudden chaos of notes:

the spinet's voice and human voices
and a shattering as of crockery.

Miss Emily's curiosity shakes a tremor across
the sun floating precariously in her teacup.

MISS EMILY

sits on a rock at the edge of a lake
she calls Looking-Pool. The water bears swallows

bellying for water-spiders, continually
adjusting their flight, like missiles

tracking targets swooping upwards like scimitars
falling like maces on heavy chains, rising upwards

like bubbles, bursting like sparks from fireworks
over the light swirling setting its marble in the water.

Miss Emily sits in silence, like soot,
a heap of fine ash the swallows fling off.

She watches the sun go deeper into its furnace.
The stars and the moon are a canvas

of the hooded eyes of inquisitors brightening
around the white, shorn head of a heretic nun.

She watches the sun slowly burn the green world brown
then soak it in blood, then cast it in black.

She sees how her hands have wrinkled finely
like a snake's back, how her joints are the neck-folds

of lizards. She senses the awesome age
of the Looking-Pool. The head on her shoulders

is dull as a turnip. She sees dark gather
thickly, like sod. Death holds Miss Emily

at the root of this dark, like a stump.
She hears the resonant chord of an owl hooing.

She strains to see the swallows, but Death
has clotted darkness with a pulsing ballet of bats.

MISS EMILY

rises from the rock
and walks through the moonlight.

A cold beauty comes touching silvertipping
turning everything to shimmer.

The glaze of the moon is a lighter liquid set loosely
on the mercury of water; a stand of trees

glistens in oils on a canvas of granite.
The world is still as mineral, solid as an abbey.

Even the clouds have drifted off in whispers
and misted softly rising in the grass.

But all muscle and mouth suddenly a fish
hurls at the surface deadcenter on target

like a stone exploding a polished window
and Miss Emily's heart smashes fiercely

at its limit of ribs but the fish disappears
from the vanishing target and the moon returns smoothly

to its zero. Death has Miss Emily think
that everything is happening

outside of her;
and the water's amen is the moon.

DEATH

leaves her in silence
standing frozen on the path,

married to boulders and blackness.
Her heart hammers frenzies slowly

like a pheasant pinned in a spaniel's mouth;
her mind reels with voices like the stokehole

of a furnace. She steadily fixes her eyes
on the small secure details of the dark's disassemblements.

Bit by bit the birds resume their notes.
A chipmunk chitters the thrill of its alarums.

The clock from the village church-spire
strikes out at the wilderness

distilling all sound
to one note.

And a rabbit that fright held
springs quickly away

getting on with what always
might be her last day.

MISS EMILY

dreams deeply of possets of rose-hips
and camomile cure-alls

while the moon softly steeps,
brews the meadows in mistiness

and the wind swirls the night like an ocean.
There is scarcely a breeze in the touch

of light in the jackpine, in the droop
of the willow-leaves dripping in the moonlight,

in the shivering of silver in the chains of the clock.
Suddenly the room is wide with silence, like an eye.

All ankles and elbows she
shuts her mouth on a shout and her heart

stops stuttering O
what is it what

A slim fish, then another: brook trout
or rainbows whirling slowly

rounding the bedposts through the window
round the willow to the Looking-Pool and gone

down without a sound into the wobble
of the deep well-mouth of moonlight.

Very still, in the reassuring warmth
of her own deep bed and her snug white nightdress,

Miss Emily feels her heart return
to normal. But her breathing is irregular.

Dreams fill her. Her body feels like water.
She feels herself dissolving, moving like light

through an incandescent mist. As from a great depth,
muffled by many doors and corridors, the clock begins

to strike the hour, pulling at its machinery.
But Miss Emily's mind is blank. She hears nothing.

MISS EMILY

turns fitfully, at the end of the night,
on the spit of her dreams.

She wakes to the scuffle of a large moth
guttering the flame of her oil-lamp.

She pulls her comforter up, bunching it.
A white rose appears. She lets its petals

be mountains and oceans. She watches a wolverine
vanish in an arctic waste of moonlight,

its muzzle jaggedly sewn around the crimson
meat of a caught, senseless rabbit.

She watches a whale's great mouth push itself
through its food. She sees an ostrich strut

its feathers on the leathers of its billy-club
feet. She feels the earth sail space slowly

in the doldrum of infinity. Queer columns of animals
slip through her fingers: they are brides-and-grooms

walking down an endless aisle where the wedding-
party's all turned to stars. A world untravelled

comes ringing her room. It is Death's gift.
It is Miss Emily's only dowry.

THE MIST

rises softly at dawn
like a turned tide. Death approaches Miss Emily

in his naval uniform. Miss Emily is in white.
She feels him rise from the Looking-Pool,

come quietly through the window and wait,
with great courtesy, at her vanity.

The room shimmers with a dark radiance.
She floats, immensely happy, away from her body.

She offers Death, politely, her life.
With a smile, and bowing gracefully,

Death refuses. He gives her immortality.
The Elements, however, don't stand

on such ceremony and claim quickly
what remains

of Miss Emily.

In Transit

(1985)

Turning Out the Light

His fear is the house
where soundlessly the cancer

roots in the humid dark,
extending its slow eyes

like the groping pale tentacles
of tubers left to rot

in warm winter cellars, moving always
towards whatever light

will sustain their life.
As it finds none

where it is,
it keeps growing.

He is allowed into the Lab
where he examines the stained drop
of his own blood, which is sunk down
at the bottom of the bright well
of the electron microscope.

Horizon to horizon, the slide
is a watercolour of great beauty:
the dark cells of the cancer
hold their own in the greens
and blues of the shifting
sea of information.

He peers down, as through
the viewfinder of a long-range plane,

coming suddenly upon a flotilla
of tiny rafts—the survivors
of some disaster taking place nearby:
they are all that remain
of whatever spawned them.

As he scans the millimetres, he sees
great courage, and will—
so fragile in the crowded wash
of so many cells.

For a moment, he doesn't know
whether to save them,
or let them drown.

In the dim half-light
of the curtained room,
subdued by drugs, he sleeps.

The dark plays tricks
with his face: his eyes
are half-open, but the sheet

shifts slightly; so he sleeps,
the steady breathing
broken only by the regular

pulsing of the heart
at the faltering end
of each breath.

It is like the faint scratch
of a bug beneath the floor.

Soon in the gathering silence
all I can hear is the rasping
scratch of the bug subsiding
then loudly gaining its hold

as if trying to break out
of the dark hole of his throat.
It is the sound of the Deathwatch

in the house of the dying,
feeding in the wood beneath the bed,
ticking like a clock until the soul leaves.

The first day, in the Common Room,
he stood in line with them,
the fifty little boys
in schoolboy grey—
a row of neat parcels
knotted at the neck
with the new School Tie,
their fathers' brush-and-polish
still gleaming on their shoes.

The Head Master ran down the Roll
as each, according to his way,
piped *Here, Sir*; when it came
my brother's turn, he
did what he could, nodding furiously
to help make the answer
fluid and cool, but the nodding
was of a fish beached and doomed
and my foolish brother fell dismal
and silent and tired of it all—

until out of nowhere
the first syllable burst and rang—
and fifty boys stood, stiffening
with astonishment, craning wide-eyed
in shifting rings of whisper
and barely-clamped lungfuls of glee.
He expelled slowly his breath.
It was the right word, and well said.

The Head was kind—and caught
quickly the sputtering agitation
in an all-ranks, eyes-front,
dense charge of silence,
under a look that would have had
the least squeak
trip his room-blast of roar. He said, quietly:
You should also say 'Sir.'

And the S began in a blush of trust,
with a tearing sound
as of long-ripping paper,
a valve not properly fitted,
as the lungs deflated slowly on and on
transfixing the Master suddenly
charmed by this hissing serpentine sway,
the long consistent unstoppable sibilants,
esses upon esses and my brother almost
out of breath, eyes closed,
every muscle tense stepping out into
the sheerfall of accelerating seconds
tongue pressed aching relentlessly
against the incontinent buzz of his teeth—
until the throat stuck shut on its glottis
and his twisted face crimsoned
at the guttering ends of exhaustion—

but the lungs refused collapse
and the bright miracle of breath came pouring
back in a deep, pure sob saying,
Sir, Sir!—and a last,
escaping, joyous, *I'm Here, Sir!*

Evenings we watch
the darkness descend
in its needle

and the morphine
rise in the drowse
of his smile

for a minute,
and a minute,
luxuriant in his skin,

becoming compound
with his body
instant after instant

in the dark
tumbling slow-motion
down, finding its depth,

losing to the air
to all even gravity
the loathsome flesh,

eyes opening wide
the zero of darkness,
until blood pounds his brain
into black.

The Deathwatch here
is not some black bug.

Neither is its home
the unwearied bedside clock
or the hopeless half-measure
of calibrated liquids
dripping down slowly through the tubes.

It is my brother's heart,
taprooting every vein
in its wasting host
to gain its each next second of life.

This always was its place;
it sits in its dark room
and ticks effortlessly on.

He is tired of the shame
of wetting his bed; he wants
the wheelchair toilet.

I sit him on the edge of the bed.
He tries one foot out in the air
and his thigh shudders with the effort.

He studies the much-laundered sheets,
the fraying seam of his terrycloth robe.
He is already shivering with fatigue.

He eases his leg back.
He manages his breath awkwardly,
like a runner too long in a race.

He can't move. His eyes glaze,
rolling up into a faint
and I catch him and hold him.

I see how difficult it is
to hold on, to keep
all the facts in mind.

How long he cries is the measure
of this one defeat. Death is now
the three-foot fall from the bed.

I am his lover
when I hold him,
careful not to turn away

without the promise
of a better place
to put his pain, a safer

minute to rest in;
I make it seem
that fear is always

elsewhere than the present
and any place at all
but there in my arms.

I am his lover
when I hold him,
not his brother.

Lunch is a spoonful
of raspberry Jell-o.

Afternoons mean sleep
or the introduction of long needles
into the breast-bone or hip,
or deep through the flesh of his back,
for a plug of liver or an extract of marrow.

The finger-pricks come twice a day.
Even the sound of the softly opening door
has him cry out and gag
on the dregs of his vomit.

Each day they
change the soaking twist of sheet.
They will continue this
until they get it right,
until the right one fits:
it will be spotless,
and dry, and neat.

When I saw him come home
from the autumn Soccer Trials,
edgy and glum that the boys on the field
were too big, I hit him on the mouth
until he bled, then kicked him for a coward
when he fell onto the floor.
He convulsed in a breathless
stuttering wail of shock.

The next week he came home grinning
muddy and bruised, telling me the news
of his team. The soccer boots hung
from his shoulders like a prize.
I went to my room, tight with shame.

When I see the syringe's slim,
savage jab, to push morphine
to just the fringes of the pain,
I remember that I too injured
to heal: but this is not
the stammering doubt
of a timid boy, or the brutal
love of his brother.

When I see his fear,
the measure of my love
is such that I could
not harm, but kill.

In his room, if he can't raise
his head from the soft down pillow,
or his back from the lamb's wool pad,
he can't reach the door.
If he can't reach the door,
he can't come back to the world.
If he can't come back to the world,
there is no hope. But this is the cell

of most hope of all:
this is the circle of hell
stocked with the staples
of hope—fine medicines, the balm
of quiet speech and light caress.
It is a safe place to lie

in the acid reek of vomit
and the stinking blurt and drool
of diarrhea. It is a harbour
to moor in, to endure
the bright flares of pain
savaging each exhausted nerve,

where every pore is a mouth
dumb with spent agony.

If he can't come back,
he is left to lie in hope,
as in a suffocating fire
that draws its life
from every breath he takes,
consuming itself, and air,
and him.

I explain it carefully to him:
it is my job, as sitter
at the deathbed, in the manner
of our conventions here
without the high Greek keening
at the sky in which the souls
of sailors vanish; or the aching
air of Arab villages
fluttering in the million
wings of ululation—though uncalled-for
these cries press at the root of my tongue
and once I wept, helpless,
helpless in the dark, while he slept.

I explain that nature
does not sleep and all nature
feeds on itself endlessly
in every patch of garden, every lake
and wisp of cloud; look, I tell him,
nothing stops, nature is a great heart
and the world is its living body
which consumes us as easily
as we consume air.
I explain it carefully,
carefully in the dark while he sleeps.

He thinks his bones
are the stainless pipes
of the bedside railings—
thin and hollow and perfectly
painless, surrounding
the broken body
of somebody else.

The mouth of his nightmare
is open wide, as for speech;
it is Death's little rictus,
the white lips a draw-string
tightened around the sack of chilled flesh
the body contains. These deadened eyes
had led the way down to the depths
in a fire of salt, frantic
to escape the thin-rubber lids
that held them in;

and now, as they watch
the calm blue light floating
above the bright sheet
of water, the body rises up
scoured by the rounding of the keel.

These walls are white doors
without handles. The surfaces
are mirrors that won't work.

The faces of these walls
are the chalk masks
of mummers come to mimic,

who've forgotten their lines
and why they came,
and he can't tell them.

Their silence is a Babel
with all its shrieking tongues
cut at the root.

Their eyes are blank, under even
the brightest light, white lids
holding darkness down perfectly.

Though I close my own eyes
and stop up my ears, still the silence
and the light, are right here.

The morning drip
eases red cells
into the bloated arm

which hangs from his body
like some enormous slug
feeding quietly at his shoulder.

The nurse's fingers
leave grooves in the underside,
and a dent in the top

where her thumb rests.
Then fluid fills the arm
and it is round again,

leaking a little pink
which pools on the sheet
at his elbow. She uses that arm

until the vein is not available;
then she uses the other arm.
Twice a day,

on the column
by his head, his life
hangs, upended.

In Recovery, he rests
cold in his cot.

The technician uses the vein
at the base of his heel
to introduce the needle
and release the drug.

The marauding cancer is scattering
against this new force. By morning,
like guerrillas melting into the hills,
nothing will be left of them
but the fear of their coming again.

We read magazines, and wait.

The bedside radiator's
wavering mirage of heat

shifts pale midwinter light
across the broad yellow curtains

and white hospital walls, slowly floating
the shadows like flowers on water.

The whisper of the air-line
still working at his mouth,

I bend down to talk,
or hold him, or wait:

floating on his body
is a flower on its bough

which a wind moves lightly through
and lifts away.

Exhausted finally by medicine,
by the tiny, nauseating stings of the needle,

he has his stammer back
and can hardly speak.
He lies caught in the maze

of his own simple bones,
in the corner of defeat
he can no longer put a name to.

His breath comes disembodied out,
like wind over a tongue
dry and thick as a lizard's;

the slow syllables falter
at the font of some mirage
the torment of his mouth
gathers air to drink from:

it is no longer his mouth,
or face, or voice.

And there is nothing there.

I touch his forehead, still warm,
in a blessing useless to anyone
but me; and brush the damp hair
out of his eyes, thinking
how extraordinary it is
that he has no breath.

Your eyes were wide open
when the world fell away,
my lovely brother.

The orderlies are quiet, efficient men
who manage the bulky marionette
of their patient's heavy body
and roll it neatly in a sheet
like an insect cocooned in a leaf,
then slide it onto their trolley.
Among the others, they had liked him,
and hesitate covering his head.
Then they roll him down the long clean corridor.

One of the rubber wheels squeaks,
catching occasionally on itself
and spinning furiously, a protest
nipping at the heels of the little parade
until they reach the scarred metal doors
of the freight lift.

They take him down seven floors
to Autopsy, where he is opened
and cut into pieces.

The mortician corners the black Seville
with one ringed finger on the wheel,

sucking Coke from a hole
he has cut in the lid
of a take-out cup.

Which bone in the box
of ashes in my lap
bumps the thin walls
with each new street?

Small runs of glue
have dripped from the top

and I can't see
how to open it,

to look.

Black box, black car
gliding through the snow;
driver sipping at the lid,
sucking at the drop,
at the bottom of the cup.

I push some snow,
some loose earth
into the small hole

and cap the hill
with a limp handful
of hot-house daisies.

They scarcely veil
the sullen face
of the dirt, at whose

crude altar I squat
to tell my loss.
Then kneel, numb suddenly

as the flowers
trying their hopeless, lovely anthem
in my head.

———

Among his things
there is a notebook on his desk,
charting December, 1976.

The first two weeks
appear in a steady hand,
the lists and plans
remarking on the details
of the daily routines
—so much medicine, so much pain,
so much sleep: the thick wall
of fact that keeps out
the chaos of fear.

The third week trembles
and seeks its proper columns.

The last week is blank.

———

His album's full of daisies,
their simple faces
obedient to his shutter.

Our own garden grew,
and flourished, and fell;
but not one shot of a blowsy rose,
or the bright red straggle of geranium.

The trains are the old ones,
the ones they use for day-trips.
He'd shoot out the window
at the churning steam-wheels
and chugging blasts of smoke,

then print up the shots
to put up on the wall.
Then frame the best stills
by his stationary bed; then the trains,
the trains were all dead.

The last in the book
is a shot he took of me.
I remember the pose: I became
the boy he thought his friend;
we didn't know each other then,
those years ago.

In the closet, his Oxford shirts
are button-down, and blue.
The papers in his briefcase say

that all his policies expire
the last day of the calendar year.
All his bills were paid on time;

and today is New Year's Day.
He kept his brown hair short, and neat.
He wore brown penny-loafers, polished,

grey pants, pressed, grey socks,
or brown, or blue, changed daily.
He wore casual sweaters, casual slacks:

He worked at his appearance
until he was almost
one of us.

He worked at his appearance
until now he is almost
invisible.

In the aeroplane home
I sink back against the huge power
of the turbines, buried in the howl
of the straining jet, one passenger
among a hundred others, fixed on the pilot's
delicate dials, the solicitous
smiles of the Tourist-Class staff.

Bone-weary suddenly of detail,
of talk, I let myself fall
in the relentless roar of lift
and turn my face to the window.

What remains is a carrying-bag, pale blue, two
tied cardboard boxes in the cargo bay,
some re-usable clothes, photographs to show
who's left, a calculator which flared once
in a frenzy of green numbers, then settled,
for the longest time, to the bright little mouth
of zero. Then a dot, very faint. Then nothing.

When they ask me what I want
I find that I can't speak.

SPRING

For Jeffrey Harris
August 3, 1946–New Year's Day, 1977

Soon a slip of garter-snakes trying their tongues
against the witch-grass and Queen Anne's lace.
And each fresh leaf a chrysalis unfurling green,
curling-to-flat its one wet wing. Slim fiddleheads
untensing in the slow yield of spring. Soon every stone

released and new as water. And not yet six months gone.
Then the young all over, searching out their note
with the dark-eyed snow-owl, master to the choir.
And the knock-kneed lambs, flimsy walk-and-totterers
for whom still the simplest answers will be riddles.

Soon large in the parish will the thunder bunch
its fists, the thunder roll its muscle
and trees fall dead. Nothing rises, Jeffrey,
as quietly as you. Not the wintering daisy
at seed in the meadow, the grace of summer fields.

Not the crow at its song, wheeling at the window.
Not the whispers (not of fear) that came
shrieking at my ear. Not the one-note whispers
you saved for New Year's Eve. No visitors, you said;
and said: Please turn the light out when you leave.

The Light-House Keeper

The steady sweep
of the minute-hand
rounds its circle of black,

its thin beam
indicating safe passage
through all disaster,

though the rocks and sea meet
and burst, settling exhausted,
an astonishment dissolving

as when your body tenses
under the moving sheen
of slippery glisten

when I lick you slowly
tracing the evanescent shiver
that runs skittering through you

until whatever seemed closed,
opens and whatever was exact
is endless. Come home.

Falling Back

Small hands prehensile and strong
in the perfect work of his body,
the baby clings to our legs.
He pokes his solemn head out
from the safety of our bodies
to look at the lake.
It is past his bedtime:
he risks nothing here

that would put him down to sleep.
As in sympathy with his
abnormal quiet, there is
still water this evening.
Even the swallows' feathery thunder
is all in the mind. They skim the surface
like visiting angels
trying the limits
of their wings.

The sole thrill is a fish, adventuring
for what in our realm walks
on the surface of his, some bug making
momentary the flash of the fish
falling back mouth-first into his shadow
as if kissing it, and the bug vanished.
Over the water, the splash
comes slow as history;
then the surface settles, perfect.

The baby cuffs a blackfly from his face,
rubs his eye. Sleep rises in him surely
as dark falls, but made bold by the bright

jump of water so far away, he totters
to the beach edge and looks out, calling.
It is cool; our own bodies shift together

in the measure of his absence. I wonder if
the fish, in that instant, saw
the three of us standing on our shadows,
watching him watching us.

At home, the evening fire
struggles from its wood,
warming the sleepers
in their separate worlds.
Flames breach the quiet air
like bright, quick fish;
I am fastened to my reflection
in the glistening floor.

My face floats, as above
water, above wood
as dark as the mud
at the bottom of the lake.
'Falling back', it's called,
in military talk, though
slowly I understand
there is no way out.

The View from the Kitchen

for Nicholas, at two

On its slender stalk, raised
an inch higher by the pulling
magnet of the world, his over-sized head
swings towards the window:

A huge truck monsters up the hill,
shivering the spring air on the glass
his flattened nose and fat hands
press against. It tickles his nose
so he whacks the window.

Then turns to kiss me full on the mouth.
'Dawg!' he shouts, pointing. 'Truck,' I tell him—
'Truck!' He hesitates. 'Fuct!' he yells.
We are both delighted with the lesson.
Abrupt, he turns back to look.

In that small body, complete
in scarcely thirty inches,
the bellows of lung balloon
and deflate, keeping patiently
the slow fire of blood
lit in his tiny veins.

The mind is slowly forging
delicate notions of Art, Music,
and Truck. In his heart
pump the rhythms of War, Mathematics;
his skin has already learned the touch
of the softmouthed comforts of love.
The truck has long vanished:

'Gheeze!' he instructs, dumping
his body at my arms; I pick him up

to get the cheese, opening wide
the bright mystery of the fridge.
He fastens tight to my neck
and leans dangerously, to get a good look,
curious about all things.
Fed, he is sad there is no noise
outside the kitchen; there is only me.

I start my motor. His joy is so pure,
I remember mine—and drive roaring slowly
through every room of the house—
for I am his, and he clings to me,
and will not be let down.

An Octopus

The creature stroked by
in pebble-mottled water,
its hide at one with the calm
of the village bay,
until with neither last whisper
nor the artful deceit of medicines,
it met death descending soundless
with its sinuous, soft-tentacled grasp,
probing with muscles focused,
delicate suddenly as fingertips
finding the core of a new lover's body.

The boy is done
with his quick plunge
of spear, pulling now
with all his fingers at the small beast
wrapped frantically about his hand.

He bangs the slack body on the granite wall
with wet loud slaps, like laundry
the women savage on the washing-rock;
it will be cut, and cooked, and eaten
while small gulls stab at its innards on the dock.

Single-minded, the bigger gulls rise
above the salt-reek of seaweed,
dropping shellfish on the stone shore
to burst their belly-full of mucus.
They settle like diners to tables and eat.

Goats, Agios Nikolaos

The small, domed building
on this sunlit hill
is slaughterhouse for the town.

Flies crawl about in three bins, feeding
on clots of blood stuck to the metal sides,
and on the still-warm stumps of the necks

of the severed heads of goats. Around the back
they've parked a cart packed with goats
flicking tails and ears—fidgeting

at the dark, strong smells, stamping
as if to sustain their years
of mountainside balance.

Inside, the damp gloom
is quiet as a hillside chapel:
the poles and metal levers on the wall

resemble the cast-off braces
of healed cripples. The cool cement floors
are freshly washed, rid

of the crud in the foetid bins
a foot outside the door.
Men are eating lunch and talking

outside in the Aegean blue, the air
perfumed by thyme and oregano, the day balmy.
The goats' heads lie with their tongues fixed tight,

ears without a flick against those flies,
eyeing with ancient eyes each other's decomposition,
those lovely fierce horns and beards and cloven feet.

The Nude Beach, Paros

The Europeans' parts dangle variously
tumescent in the heat, or shrunk by the sea,
nipples shrivelled pebble-small,
then bloomed back to laxity.

The lolling breasts bake, indolent
in the slow range of sun;
the water's salt cap tightens
stickily on stiff hair.

How different they seem at first,
then how all the same: the sand grinds
along each limb, the grit's in each crease
and the talk's all small, no matter

what tongue it finds expression in.
These bodies make their world
at the factory, or run it from the office.
Now the sea is their road of gold

and the Parian marble hills
are the glittering walls of Heaven.
They have gathered their dishevelled selves
and reduced them to the one dumb body,

healing hourly on the beach.
Mindless, happy, the horizon
lapping at their feet, they curl up
neat as the stillborn in bottles

warmed on the laboratory's sunlit sill, dozing,
dozing at the edge
of the end of the world.

The Watchmender, Paros

Something's broken,
and they don't know what.
These are the watches
their grandfathers brought—
the springs so thin now
they'd snap at his touch:
and they expect them fixed.

Under the small shop lamp,
his two differing eyes work hard
against each other: the clear one
fastened to his optic lens—
the wayward other, wandering with disuse,
dimly taking in the villagers
whose shadows pass his window,
or stand before him, waiting.

He bends like a priest
by the deathbed candle,
to attend to the useless glow
of jewels sunk deep
in almost-dead works,
like rosaries of stars
that won't wear out.

From the Hotel Calypso, Corfu

The sky floats slowly shifting
its freight of stars and the dark
drains finally from my balcony

and from my bed. Boys drive by
the hotel gate, throttling their scooters,
revving hard the hot, small engines.

They've dropped off girls
whose breasts press still
lightly into their backs,

and whose goodnight touch of kiss
was a memory before it happened.
They gun their wild bikes and are gone

reluctantly into small rooms, machines
tucked cooling underneath their windows.
In the rooms next to mine, the girls lie back

in the cool of their sheets,
with the breeze still on their cheeks,
and the engines buzzing still between their legs.

Underneath the steady presence
of the distant summer moon,
the transformer drones at its lines.

Constitution Square, Kerkira, Corfu

Small fish feed
where the sewage pipe ends,
running like a root
past the Old Town quay

and emptying out into seawater.
The odour rises
into the evening Square,
into the perfumes

of aftershave and oleander
where the boy-men parade
in too-tight pants—
cocks of the walk

near the girl-women talking
careful of their looks
and laughing in front
of the carriages of infants

in charge of widowed grannies,
and the smoking elders
behind them all,
like wraiths of goatherds

with headstrong flocks.
Here too are the dead,
twisted in black cloth
about the arms of the men,

shrouding the women
in drab black dresses;
and the unborn await
their time in the town's

mixed airs, in the rolled-up
sleeves of the strutting
young men, and the long black hair
of the women.

By the Green-Fig Tree

Mornings I take the baby
down to the washing stream
where the women work
by the oleander bushes
and the green-fig tree.

Dust from the dry town road
settles softly on all they wash;
but their eyes are on the baby,
laughing and calling for him,
calling and scrubbing and laughing.

They wring their hard week out
with the water of the wash;
though the dust that falls, falls
lightly, lightly, the baby's glee
runs clear for them as upstream water,

and they kneel renewed
in their thin black dresses,
in the pink and the green
of the oleander bushes
and the green-fig tree.

His Daughter

Her head inclines to each soft tug
until all the waves of curl are caught
and bound in a sure, tight splice—

though her friends dance on the dock
slipping through the dusk, calling out
by the baskets of senseless fish.

They sit apart, these two, and take a long time
talking quietly in the boat, though the man's speech
slows as he feels the familiar pull at his hand.

His own friends finish their stitching
and coiling, mending nets and lines,
and call him for drinks to the bright café.

He attends to her talk with twelve years of patience
above the cradle of the sea which bears them
still in its slow-breathing bed

and lullabies now, with lisp and whisper
the small boat's hull, until the red trim darkens
and the red hull fades, running like blood into the water.

When the last of the light falls, scattering in the harbour,
then she bursts away, dancing happy in the dark,
hauling that laughter hard through his heart.

The Dolphin

Above the milling oyster-gatherers,
on the rise of the hill the corrida bull
anchors in long lance-grasses,
dipping leisurely at the green cape

of fodder, content with cud and sun.
Ants rummage at his feet,
through the one remaining eye
of a pelican, running their conveyor-belt

the length of its dead beak, then
gone with their loot into the slow-
boiling cauldron of the beach.
The boys grind long metal bars

into the back of the reef, prodding
among the decomposed million shells
for what life the sea sustains;
low tide, they poke at the rock

chipping flakes of shell away,
slipping carefully the mouthfuls of oyster
into plastic sacks for their supper.
The clean slice of the dolphin's fin

rises and falls, the flat tail-flukes
like the wings of a solitary angel, sailing
easily through the boys' wild yells, their hard-
thrown skippingstones and oyster-shells.

The Road of the Dead

The way home leads
past roadside shrines
of plastic flowers stuck in tins
rusted by seawater and the winter rains,
the yellow petals faded
one shade a day towards the light.

At dusk the souls rise
flittering up from the garbage
and the rat-rustled
litter of the roadside.
In the tidal cove a caught skate
flounders in the shallows—a powerful
frantic bellyflopping slap
at the vanishing surface of the water;
out to sea, the flying fish
tiptoe momentarily
above some running torpedo of hunger,
then fall back lightly
into the mouth of the sea.

Tin shacks rot in the shadows
of great herons singing
their awkward hosannas.

A delicate egret presides
at some feast on the ghost-ridden shore.

New and Selected Poems

(1992)

Spring Descending

Let me correct something before
I begin, for I know what I am
about to do. I am about to enter
you, a room full of people

prepared to adopt whatever face
I adopt to enter the room with.
If I shift this profile to suit
what I think will suit you, this

room of people I haven't yet
met, then I am nobody and you
will make of me whatever you wish.
As I am guileless, so will you be

beguiled. I am nobody:
that is how I will enter you.

———

Now she swings out banging behind her
the screendoor, which should alert the
whole neighbourhood to her beauty barely
contained by her pink bathing suit.

Thumbs through Joyce's *Portrait of the Artist*
as a Young Man. Someone closer to her
own age. I was that young once.
Examining those pages before she was even born.

She lets me do with her as I wish.
She cooks my supper and makes my bed.
I am sore confused; she lets me come
she lets me go and thanks me

this afternoon of spring descending into summer.
I am lost I am found I am lost O Lord.

The difficulty is to let her hair
stray across her forehead down over
her cheek and not want
to brush it away, to see her face clearly

as in a photograph that will
remember perfectly for me. I try to remember
the moment exactly as it happened,
condemning it to life diminishing always.

The more I fear I will not be able
truly to remember, the more I fear,
and the more I will forget.
She will come back to me

in pieces, forever. I say forever—
but I think it gone already.

Children have begun to gather even now
in the circus of the schoolyard,
courting each other patiently
with dandelions and broken sticks.

Some skip rope, innocent of the music
the skipping makes. Some sing.
The same songs every spring rising,
the same songs falling with the coming of the snow.

My place is to make this music
as if I don't need her here—

though I give whatever I can,
turning always back towards her with open eyes.

Elsewhere the children wait,
pulling out roots, tearing off branches.

———

Were I to live for sleep, to rise simply
to ascend the carousel, to ride out
the roundelay of do, done, yet to do—
while every ordinary ripple in the kitchen sink

becomes the wave curling murderous
over drowned Atlantis, the parting of the seas
for Moses and his grief-begotten tribe—
then she would have no place.

But as it is, her promise holds
of calm waters, that ineffable silence
at the heart of all my little noise.
Were I to live for her, I'd rise

into the familiar air of my own room happily,
sweeping dust from the floors, wiping the windows clean.

———

This little bubble I've urged into being,
this toy soap-pipe miracle let go
and falling, let go and rising
in the whim of the slightest wind,

this neverending round of prayer I've spun
from the wheel of my broken breath—
this whimsy of light in the fragile
gypsy-crystal hovering over the table—

is this the true thing—this
finally floating thing she's
caught the end of the string of
with the tips of her fingers? No matter

how it turns to rise away, it is her
holding it back that urges it up.

———

The music accompanying this
is at first the spring-door
whacking back into place
and a crow shouldering off up

towards the stave of powerlines
in an air grey and cool—
a solitary note diminishing in the quiet
of light now falling into her hair

at ease on her shoulder,
into the full, sudden focus
of her eyes on mine saying
for this very moment I am

yours. I am, at last, at peace—my little craft
adrift, the storm gone out to sea.

———

Feeds me supper. Jumps up to see
the sunset, a shed snakeskin, what it was
the woodpecker was jabbering at.
Out in a flash to sunbathe

for a languid hour, collecting all the calls
of birds she doesn't know

the names of, the noise of a chainsaw,
an idling telephone van with a young man

eating his lunch in the cab, caught
by the sunbather reclining where
the sun is richly focused;
where the world has suddenly focused:

it is grackle, finch, white-throated
sparrow. Tamarack, basswood, wild rose.

Other things go about their lives
simply; that is, there are
now buds in a red mist
hanging aloft in the maples,

millions of maples, millions
of buds misting in the air
which in a week will break
into green along the highway

that took us here from town.
And will bring us back, but
not now, not for a day or two,
please God, my face has thawed

and I am capable of sight, my senses
all my senses have come back to me.

I arranged the rooms with care
to deceive her. Not one dead hair
remains on the rim
of the porcelain sink.

The mouth she turns
to kiss me with now
is wet and clean and sweet-smelling.
It is the mouth all men want.

It is the garden I enter
under the broken calliope
of birds arranging their rings
above a doomed man whose penis

is a flower offered up
to tender her love.

Uninvited, two woodpeckers tap on two trees,
two simple tattoos to awaken me—not to
awaken me at all, though they do. The sun, too,
could have done it in this run-on

world nothing I can do stops.
She took her sleeping shirt off
in the night and her shoulder lies alive
in light that barely reaches it, though the light

goes as easily as it comes and she
turns away from me in her sleep
taking shoulder and light and my
temporary pleasure. Then the birds stop,

having something else in mind. What's left me
is her body, breathing quietly, to fill the silence up.

It is a little world, this—
the refrigerator humming in its

unison in the cabin settled
under the hum of the powerlines

among the riven arms of trees, their
lives about to be put on
in green and red and sunlight.
If I am very careful

I can keep this simplicity.
I mean I can keep this focus
outside towards the slow gathering
of trees in the grey light free of ghosts

and monsters and panic. And then there she is—
humming off-key something from *The Magic Flute* at the sink.

She is stripping the bed, singing.
The stripped beds of lovers should
always be sung to, the room a cathedral
for anthems floating from the mouths of boys,

the barroom grinding its dance
from the bodies of sweating women,
the whoop escaping riders on the rollercoaster
when the world hangs motionless and far away

before the descent begins. She is opening
curtains and windows, the summer light
rushes in everywhere, nosing about and settling
content in its new place. The room of the lovers

is the choir's breath gathered under the maestro's little stick,
at the edge of the plunge of the very opening note.

This is her time of evening: the darkening lake
in watercolours for barely ten minutes,
then black, and our faces in the black of the cabin window.
I am beginning to number things: ten minutes

for this one look at the lake; three days for the
two of us. Were there one thing to do, to make
time stop, I'd do it. But one thing only
would form the first of an inevitable list,

the evanescent vision melting image-by-image
into nightmare. She turns her face
from the window, picks up a book, and reads.
I am left with the lake, the watercolours dissolving

into an impression of my own face at the window.
Behind me the careless pages turn and turn.

The white-throated sparrow hangs
the whole night on its song, the whole
spring beginning in that simple air.
In the bedroom, she's pulled the warm silk

of a blue kimono over her: it pools in folds
of bright water falling over cooling skin,
over the quiet bed. Such stillness now in the whisper
of her hairbrush, the belt recomposed

into an orderly knot, her body gathered neatly in
as if it hadn't cried out, hadn't jerked
and surged in that soft violence we wanted
and watched enter us, and take us, and leave.

Then the world returned, wind and leaf,
in the after-echo silence of the singing bird.

The fields were half-green,
half-grey on the way here.
I saw mostly the mist of green
coming up from the ground—

and that red misting the trees—
not that my seeing the green and the red
did anything to alter what
was there at all but I call what I saw rising

a good sign. Also good is her
warmth, which has little to do
with me, but which rises
under my hand on her belly

as if it wants to. It doesn't really,
but I take it as a gift anyhow.

I bought sunglasses today. It happened
at a clothing store where racks of T-shirts
for women hung in an ice-creamery of colours:
raspberry mousse, pistachio, chocolate royale.

The men's were more direct: black, white,
forest green, navy blue: colours of substance.
On the other side of my new sunglasses, the whole store
lacked any real colour whatever. I feel a metaphor

welling up here. A metaphor, God must have thought
as He blew dust in various nostrils or had Eve
spring whole from Adam's rib, is a powerful
thing and the first step to an understanding of things

as they really are. Tomorrow, when I dress, methinks I'll tape
two fresh lemons to my chest, go forth, and multiply.

It is because I am tired, I tell myself,
that I can hold nothing that's
not a cliché to candle
against the light of the page—

and can give her nothing
of use but my attention
for the days we have together—
but haven't really, when I think about it,

think that I can scarcely hold
a moment still, face to face
with itself, mouth to mouth—
although her body takes mine in

and draws from it what it can—as against
that old cliché of making love itself.

Back to town, to my resident centipede. It slithers
all its parts up the landlord's thin layer
of fresh paint, all esses and legs behind

the intelligent dot of its head. I've taken
to jabbing at it but it snakes through cracks
from which later it will emerge and attack me.

I'm bored. I want her here. I've installed a clock
above my desk. The brisk finger skims through
the minutes in its perfect face, dragging the slow

hours with it. She will burst through the door
even though it's very late to kiss and kiss and kiss
me. I am suffering other absurd notions, stuck wafting

like a weed between the surface-noise and the deep
sea-swell, numb. Watching the clock turn purring
like a sleeping cat. Waiting for the centipede. And her.

Let me alter the myth to fit
what in fact happened: she patted
the wax into place, saving the honey
for whatever else she had in mind,

tired of having me tag along, disappeared
in one great closing of her wings,
and left me to the labyrinth
with nowhere to go but up.

With thinning air to hold me
one wingbeat from grace, I traced
her path into the fire
until my head burst into flames

and I began the fall.
And in my growing shadow saw
the awful chaos of the sea
alive with plenitudes of fish

breeding and devouring, in water whose
softest body was about to turn
to stone. Perhaps the story
hasn't changed at all:

I see the simple truth is:
once I flew. And once I fell.

The Goddess (I)

She squats in stone at the top
of the church-door arch, compact as a monkey

in the crotch of a jungle tree, momentarily
safe, like a wound freshly under its dressing.

Underneath that gap-toothed skull
her crude fingers reach around her buttocks

and pull herself open.
It is the entry to the cave

of the Oracle at Delphi,
whose answers emerge through the dark

in the shape of red mouths glossed
in the perfumed cling of lipstick;

whose every revelation clicks out
over the sidewalks on high heels.

In the dark-rimmed blanks of her eyes
the dot of a baby rises spinning, alive,

breaking bald as the moon through torn cloud,
for this stone beast is the mother of us all.

Siren Songs

It is where the water rises to
fall against the rocks the problem starts
and ends. The Song of the Sirens is one

I'm familiar with. It begins innocently
enough, a kind of *mmm*-ing in the middle
of making love, though it doesn't stop there.

Hard on its tail, as when the doctor
inserts his stick, is the opened-wide *aah* which
rises on up the scale to a full-throated wail

an octave beyond what is held
to be proper in drawingroom company
which is where the drowning happens.

The sailor who plugged his ears up and lashed himself
to the mast had the right idea. Bondage of any sort
is one way of dealing with it. But even

with wax in your ears, the silence of the cry
is deafening, the undulating of the sea relentless,
your fragile craft trying its single-handed best

to keep upright. Anyhow it's not the song itself
that terrorizes: it's the incidental imagery—
the splayed feet unconscious and white

as an upturned frog's; the belly of a fish lolling in the slops.
The jellyfish breasts. Ach. Fiddlesticks. Pythagoras had it
right when he took the measure of that scale,

bent on controlling the music entirely. He
controlled nothing. And Ulysses should've leapfrogged
the railing, jumped happily in among the fish

opened his throat, and roared. As it was,
he returned to ever-patient Penelope and died
of boredom in the arid monotone of marriage.

Epithalamion

Approaching the shrine of their marriage,
the limbs of paralytics began to twitch.
They were almost able to walk without their canes.

Under the opening thunder of chords, the deaf
began their humming,
still a little off-key. The blind peered fiercely
at the twining of the roses,
following their noses.

All about, there was great trafficking in noise.
The unborn gathered in algebras of number
and sat down to nibble at their table.
Everyone was invited. Especially the dead—
for in the betrothed the dead live happily
and were about to satisfy
their boundless nostalgia.

They brought bulimics to their kitchens
and let them wait at the ends of every line.
They clothed the beautiful in unscented deodorant
and sat them shivering naked in the wings.
The very rich were the hosers of the garden
and deliverers of juices made from concentrate.

Those of sour breath regained clean tongues
and babypink gums and the habit of flossing.
They were surrounded by acquaintances.
Shy people got up when it was time to dance
and rubbed their chests against each other, vigorously.
The mean in spirit continued to mouth off loudly,
but their complaints were as the songs of angels.

Horses were entitled to speak on behalf of the groom,
though with limited vocabularies. Cattle took the part
of the bride, and were capable of an elemental music

restricted to the blowing of kazoo tunes
through applications of coarse grass
to the large spaces between their teeth.

Snakes finally endeared themselves
to the institution of marriage, becoming
Staffs of Life. Several at a time
braided and buttered themselves, eased into the oven
and writhed slowly and swelled, smelling sweet as muffins.

Her relatives found the flowers for her hair
among the treasures of the sea, or
dropped from the beaks of seabirds, or
trailing from the backs of flying fish. Or
maybe they just found them lying around somewhere.
Warthogs shuffled up truffles for boutonnieres.
Goats handled the giving of the rings.

The cake was iced with creamed garlic
to cure the assembled's various diseases,
especially the sexual, invisible and otherwise.
Then, when everything was about to fall apart,

they were married on the boulevard
in the middle of traffic,
announcing that in this one matter
there was little room for choice, as for once
their hearts were vicissitudinistically whole,
and their bellies contained multitudes.

The Sun Rises

Sour-breathed, too sleepy
for any appropriate touch,
they fondle each other awkwardly

too early in the morning, awakened at five
by the salt-air and light flowing in
through the broad motel windows

they were too drunk to shut the previous night.
Lie there, unsettled, ten yards from the sea's
seemingly natural turns drawing curtain after curtain

on its own endless wash of applause, in artless rehearsal
that mimes the final play itself.
Above the motel, the sun rises steady as a spot

shining on the ocean's virtuoso performance,
on all that's effortless
and good at it.

A Visit to the Galleries

He has them dancing there as if
there were no end to breath,

no end to the shining oils that draw
light down and hold it in their hair.

They are in love with the moment
and will never leave it, those limbs so

carefully akimbo in the dance-hall light,
under studio lamps those evenings the moon falls

elsewhere on snowfields that would turn even the blond
summer of their skin blue and ghostly though how they

lift their bodies over the green fields here
and fling breath out into the evening air

as if there were no end to breath
and the light of day were not ephemeral.

After Matisse's *La Danse* (1909)

He caught her just in time, falling—
as clearly she was—slowly asunder.
And quickly cast her several remaining parts
in a body he arrested in the process
of dispersal, so that half her knee is lost,
her arms fallen completely off; but her belly
and full trunk still manage the life

that life wants further to remove from her.
Even the stone seems to want her
to sink down into it, beyond whatever
miracle could stop it. So now he has her
pulled relentlessly down, left alone
to incline her solitary ear
to earth, to listen to whatever will prevent
the unthinkable from happening.

After Rodin's *Inner Voice (The Muse)* (1896)

Indeed she has a very large head.
She may well have been enormous in most respects
but one or two. She might have had a small
mind, for instance, hidden behind those blank eyes
so driven back into her head by whatever it was
she didn't want him to see. Who knows, perhaps
she was tiny, though how he
must have striven to make her
huge enough to look at
closely, to study the details—but with
every magnification, every multiplication
of scale, see how she shrank back so impenetrably
to something singular, to something
as simple as metal, and that strong.

After Rodin's *Large Head of Iris* (ca. 1908)

Hay or scrub or something
blotched in, in the foreground,
without detailing; though each of those
fields of crops had a name and a human face
for whomever made a whole life there.

The brunt of all of it blocked crudely in.
The sketchiness necessary, the string
of farmhouses hinged one on the other,
an extended family of windows, doors
through which he might have walked
could he get that close, had he
been asked, would he have gone.

The houses cling to each other and the grass
shifts, endlessly settling, as if uncomfortable.
Most telling is the empty horizon:
the sky left blank of everything but primer.
That starkness of sky all over, where God might
have been, or the sun doing something to redeem
that nothing, that staring of the solitary's eye.

After Van Gogh's *Farms Near Auvers* (1890)

Everything else in this room
falls about the lovers, their

bodies risen out of the marble
like gods released at last

from the depths of the sea;
and who, with one kiss, fresh

as the very first, but forever,
cling to each other oblivious

of schoolchildren giggling
too loudly in their shadow, the couples

whose fingers thread jealousy together,
the Art Students coolly sketching

their distance; and a young man there,
in terror to look upon such work

as if his own heart's flesh
could ever become that stone.

After Rodin's *The Kiss* (ca. 1882)

The rest of her body
is round, flesh-soft and alive

as the apple she cups lightly in her hand.
But there is a hard set to that mouth.

And her nose perks up too sharply.
She has caught a little whiff of something.

The body says *I am full. I am complete.*
This is what I am. But the mouth says

Hunger. It will feed when it wants.
It has all the time in the world.

After Renoir's *Venus Victorious* (ca. 1916)

It isn't ground he is
shuffling wearily over: it is blood.
No light is anywhere implied but by those
watery shadows leaking from their trees
and stalking him across their own red earth.
One of them runs from the heels of that
stoop-shouldered, featureless, beaten man—
not man, but shadow dense enough momentarily
to gather into a man, that cane a sad flourish
in front of him, dowsing the blood, the other
hand gripping his travelling bag, that painter's
tired black case hiding instruments
once used to plumb light itself.

After Francis Bacon's *Study for a Portrait of Van Gogh IV* (1957)

Killing the Beast

After Raphael's Saint George and the Dragon *(1504–1506)*

The trick is to have the viewer engaged
in a suspension of disbelief. On the surface of it,
surely our eyes are seldom deceived—but the rest
of our senses? We should be made to feel like children
about to walk naked through a forest at night.

*

I've scaled the creature's hide, as for use
in water; winged it for air; given it
claws to indicate its power over
whatever else crawls on the earth.
I think of the body as black fire.

*

Not a bird but in the winged beast;
not any beast that walks upon the earth
but in its black claws; no fish swims in any fish's
skin but in the scales chainmailing that armoured hide.
Even the plants are the renderings of Botany.

*

Apostles to the act, an even
dozen trees stand neat
and trim against the mild,
mid-summer sky and not a cloud
in all of Christendom.

Her little church of fingers tells her attitude
of prayer under the needle of the steeple in the background;
and to the fat, phallic block of the Knight's castle tower;
and finally, to her God, who appears
to have vanished somewhere in the middle distance.

*

I wanted to have his face seem pacific, benign—
saint-like. Something to surprise in one so young.
I wanted it to seem the measure of his righteousness
in whiting out the monster of the dark. True, I've left
the halo a little thin to crown such a fierce act.

*

I've tried to make the painting faithful
to what we know is real: to retain the flawless white,
the horse obeys perfectly under the threat of those golden spurs,
else the pall of blood would undo everything
I've wanted to make clear here.

*

The boy spits the black, compacted energy
of the beast at the very mouth of the cave.
As if it would ever willingly leave that dark,
warm place. But that's the way it is with light.
The girl's already on her knees. She's next.

This is, principally, a parable about the taming of the beast;
but I've also undone the power of the Heavens and made the sky
benign and mild blue. In like fashion, the seas I've reduced
to a pond. It's an arrogance of sorts, I suppose, to have
done so, but I wanted to slow it all down enough to look at.

*

I've bound the young man in armourer's steel. I daresay
it'll fit him better later, when the parish artisans
reduce him to stone, to ready him for the rest
of the tomb—those centuries of lying perfectly
still with his lady....

*

It's odd to think that I've given so much time
to something that essentially celebrates death.
Though I did paint the horse's hooves
as raised aloft in a sort of blessing
offered by one helpless creature to another.

*

Something came upon me in a dream the other night:
'What arrogance to make one picture of one town,
one Knight in white, one Lady in her gown ...'
And the lance is the link between Beauty
and the Beast? And Death is the key to Virtue?

You posit primal answers, you get
primal questions back. My field notes ask
the unanswerable: who is the young man,
the young woman, the beasts? Who are they
all doing this for, in the first place?

*

I have her averting her eyes: the paradox is
that she'd really be looking directly at God,
as she'd see it, for her God would be everywhere.
The boy, on the other hand, is focused on his lance.
Which of them, I wonder, is present truly for the other?

*

There was one point at which I suffered
the mild temptation to float a little boat about
in the middle of the pond, stock it with a sailor
writing verses to the girl, maybe
have a Goddess hovering somewhere overhead …

*

Such a whey-face, moon-face, such a halo
of impenetrable acceptance of everything
simple and pure and right. God! What to do with her
face? Hold it up so fiercely to the light
that it would blacken, and burst, and burn!

*

I'd say God directed this, or spoke to me, if it were true,
but it wouldn't be my place to say anything of the sort anyhow,
though inasmuch as they relate correctly to all the other colours
in the picture—in the world, for that matter—the colours I tried
hard to get *right*. A lot depends on the light, of course.

Family Album (1)

I thought you might have been dead to the world—
but there you were, Father, floating unsteadily up
from your blue wing-backed chair, barely able to rise
into the celestial light of late-night television,

and there I was, braving a winter drive for some touch of you,
hesitating at the last to knock on your livingroom window,
grinning and grinning my family-album face into the glass and all
the while you rose away from me like a ghost into the blue light

to fetch yourself a little something from the sideboard. How long
did I stand there before I gave up, gave myself back to myself,
almost intact? Drove slowly off again into the snow, the avoiding
words you'd bring home daily over years of Rounds at the Hospital

—that little verse you finally reduced the world to following
me anyhow back into the night, that incantation housed safely
in the foreign tongue you use to distance yourself from whatever
deaths you can't prevent, from the living whose unassuageable

needs would crack your heart and which now render you
nightly numb-drunk. It was my turn to try just then, wasn't it?
To utter the one word that would crush us.
'Quelques nouveaux-nés,' you'd've said, *'quelques décédés.'*

Family Album (2)

The father is the ringmaster in the blare of the band,
among the balloons, the dreams of dung
and saw-dust and the trapeze-girls flying.

The boy climbs unsteadily up on the seat,
an animal perched on its first awkward barrel
to start the world's slow spinning, pushing

hard at the pedal on the wheel. The father's
the measurer with all the grids set for
the treadmilling creature to hurry to exhaustion

though there are no maps available
to gauge the distance by, just
pension cheques and cigarettes and the whirring

kitchen clock, for he was the workhorse, now set free
from the towpath rope, and there is the
first block pedalled, the wobbly

road, the corner tilted and gone. And his own father
moving behind the curtains of his room, that hand
upon his back, the set-speech, then the awful letting-go.

The Music of the Caterpillar

My song in the morning floats out in high register,
wide and clear as sunlight. In the shadows of the mango trees
bright flowers ripen and flare. All the day long, all my selves
move shiftless as butterflies through moonlight,

flying as children fly on solitary nights, skimming the endless
flowerfield of sea. In the evenings I fall to rest
on the tip of my little hill. Under my feet,
the jungle surges and subsides, blossoming everywhere

with animals. Come dusk, I alter entirely.
I am the caterpillar, sunk on the glum
stump of its torso. I wedge a mouth organ
deep into its toothless maw, and blow.

The Steward

I serve: It is my place
to give you what you want—
although my especial knack

is to set the bouquets in bowls
so well they seem richer
than the garden you grew them in.

When you come—or go—
is of little interest to me:
My place is always here.

Whatever effort I make
at doing things properly
I am rewarded more than amply for:

Everything I polish well
I see my own face in.

The Saints

We have confined them to small rooms
and narrow beds. They have to live in silence, but with
mice breeding hourly in their walls. Though our furnaces
steam fullbore through the night, we keep

the rooms of the saints very cold.
For solace, they look through the cellar keyhole
at the lost souls roaring at the light
which plasters them helplessly to the ceiling.

Their beds are also much too short.
Their legs are numb to the ankles,
and cold to the knees: they hang bulbous
off the bed between severe iron railings,

paling in the cold like winter squash
hung over the parking-lot fence
in the last farmers' market of the year.
For their despair, the saints endure hopelessly

thin electric heaters popping their vertebrae
on the long rack of winter. For comfort, they listen
to the ineffable voices of water ascending, then
descending screaming into the dark gargle of pipes.

When the cold's at their thighs,
they no longer reproduce. Soon, they can't eat.
Their hearts, like those of jilted lovers, begin by degrees
slowly to cool, as when the first flush of lava

enters finally the open body of the sea.
Their eyes take on the granite look
common to all the saints. Even the hair becomes numb.
But they are different than we are:

we thought they were dead, but they were sleeping,
only sleeping. When they wake, they tell us
what they saw in their fevers. We see mostly how
all their extremities wiggle, and return to pink.

The Siesta of the Mediterranean Man in America

Your Mediterranean Man enjoys siestas,
closing his dark-brown eyes with
thick lids which operate like
photoelectric cells, very sensitive
to the light off the seas of Italy and Greece,
near the beaches of which he wakes before dawn,
thence to his wife and various other employments
doing nothing really remarkable all day long.
Except, one imagines, during his siesta,
when his eyes are on automatic
and he is his own man. Yet this
is not always entirely the case.
He finds himself suddenly in a cold snap
(the first he has seen), trying to fire
the almost-dead battery of the family car.
As he shrugs the door closed, the hinge
cracks off at the root, and a snowflake
lands perfectly on the handle. These
are signs: the gods of the area,
in their circuitous way, are trying
to tell him something. It is not his place
to meddle with them, or to understand. Still,
two things are clear: he's got
to get that door fixed if he's
to survive in this wilderness;
and that snowflake, for all its melting whimsy
is neither bleached starfish
nor the long-frozen tear of the Madonna
to whom the men of the Mediterranean kneel daily
and give thanks. It is also clear
that the moon outside seems pure sea-phosphorous
brimming in its bowl and, upon occasion, a sea-urchin
caught in the tide of the dark, waiting patiently
for daybreak and the normal resumption of services.
That it is tangled in the bristles of an American pine
makes sense only to the man awake: and from noon
to two, he's not; he's somewhere else.

A Specialty Shop

The trout hang suspended, as in air,
nosing against the air-filter tube
like Chinese paper kites

strung to look like fish, the fins feathering,
the bone feather of their delicate spines
a still soft cooling liquid glass pulled

from the heart of the fire
and laid under rainbow-disappearing
skin, the flush of red running

under cloud broken into pieces
in the toss of surface water.
Their bellies a print of the pebbles

stippling the dark stream bed.
The slow and endless correction of dorsals
and pectorals. The mouths working

in the bubbling oxygen through the bellows of gill
in a tank beside an abacus
of barbecued chickens spinning slowly

in their own cooking fats, their own juices
draining out of holes in their throats,
the little wings like fins in their strange aquarium.

Janus

I was six, troubled by the smell
of antiseptic lotion making sodden the landscape
of bandages containing the remnant
of my mother's cancerous stomach.
My father's anguish mixed with the scent
of his oiled hair, his shaving lather, his pipe.
I knew about smell then, but not grief—
other than his for his loss, and my mother's
at her losing us all forever.

I clung hard to his girlfriend on his sofa
in his flat, as a block away in the hospital
my brother died. I drank a bottle
of champagne, as it was New Year's Eve.
I met grief, briefly, and held it:
the girl's I took to be one of the varieties of love.

Dismal list: last week the doctors kept me
outside in the corridor near my father's room
while they suctioned the faeces from his belly.
This is the way of their world: that I can't be
near the dying animal of his body, though his body
is mine, and the least grief wants to be a shared thing.
The electricity of his limp hand was the inarticulate
release of love, a little fear, nothing else.

But yesterday, set free temporarily
from the complicated silks of the marital bed,
at last I felt it, felt grief, forty-three years of it,
its orgasm bursting in a girlfriend's body
in which I made, for the first time, the true
and fleeting acquaintance of joy.

June

It's an old lie: June undone from the blindfold
of the rest of the months of the year, standing there
blinking, still tethered straining at the post,

and around its feet cool snakes unball, their black tongues
dowsing the bullfrog's whump which wells from the rotting
sump of the swamp. And there in the shimmering underseas

of new field grass, small animals flicker by like fish.
Up from the fluttery green silks of Summer, a cardinal rises
like a freed heart, heading South. The startle of a poppy

is the small red star escaping the doomed man's mouth.
The called-to-parade are the reeds, bent on keeping
their simple attention, their soldier-rigid sway.

This is part of it, the necessary fiction, as effortless
sunlight drills damp rock, and navigators' stars
flash and vanish from the blue map of June.

Circus

(2011)

The Bearded Lady

I shaved, once. All over. Took a lover
much younger than me—and not for his
conversation. I wanted the feel of a tongue
running over a mouth, slowly—but not
his tongue over my lips, nor mine over his:
I wanted his whole body licking like a tongue
over every new surface of mine. Trouble was,
my stubble. The kid got rug-rash. Carpet-burn.
By the end of the night, the boy looked—uncooked.
When his own sweat began to roast him in salt
he fled to the showers. Haven't seen him since.

Some time later I married a man
with a skin condition. The soft moss of my belly,
the fur on my face—all titillate the scaly
hide of The Alligator Man. I'm prickly and hirsute.
He's tough as shoe leather. Neat,
how things turn out.

Weary Willy

What a plodding
life I have. The wife says
'Willy get up,' but I say 'Nope,
I don't think he can.' Still,
the show goes on and she hauls me up
from bed and stands me up. 'Lethargy's
monument to itself,' she says, 'absolutely
useless.' The doctor tells me
my condition is the first case in history
of a man seeing the world sideways,
which is what lying on my side on the couch
does to watching television, is make it
perpendicular eventually and therefore the world,
when I stand up, is sideways, that is, when the wife
stands me up. The doctor himself
was horizontal at his desk, so who's to tell
who was first.

My act is: I walk across the big tent
floor slowly. This takes three hours,
same as the show. Everybody sees me
walk across the floor, but if they could get
inside my head they'd see that sideways
I am just trying to keep my balance
like one of those rats in a treadmill
walking to keep up with the ground
spinning under its feet. Except, like I said,
sideways. 'Bone idle
and useless,' says the wife, but what does she know.
I am just trying to slow things down
so it's the circus going round,
not me.

The Cupboard Is Bare

I.m. A.C.

We have gone into the poet's house and found the kitchen bare.
Not a mouse-turd of comma, not one peppercorn full-stop.
He is bankrupt of the wherewithal to hear the penne drop.

Gone the moths that flew like muses when he burned the midnight oil.
Gone the sunlit daily bread of books on the windowsill,
the tongue-loosening whisky of company come for a meal.

Gone the bouillabaisse of gossip. The manly meat of talk.
Not a simile left to dog us, nor any metaphoric cat. All his passion
cobwebbed in the corner. All our pleasure dust on the floor.

Elsewhere midwives tend to their glistening aubergines;
jewellers' pomegranates gleam in a ruby of grenadine.
Cauliflowers blanch under the neurosurgeons' care: but here—

not a fork to poke nor a knife to slice nor a cleaver to cut things out.
Not a skewer in the drawer to string them back together.
Not a draught of thought left anywhere

but it's gone down the kitchen sink.
Gone back to Scotland, to cold rock and bare hill
and pibrochs full and emptier than the grave.

The table's an empty altar
with its supplicant of chair,
when the cupboard is bare.

Speech

When I had teeth, no accent at all
was safe from me. I'd Irish groined
and turd and tank-you Lard.
I'd Scotch the ballads
wherein those drowning lords
were richt laith
to weet their cork-heeled shoon.
I'd do Canadian if I knew how—
but settle now for American, its
boo-jhwah Appalachiania,
that drawl y'all git from The Tee Vee.
Still, I'd like to report my love-life hasn't suffered.
In flagrante, I moan like a camel at stud,
a moose with no teeth, a cleft-palate dog.
Thank God I can croon the word Love.

Hoodiddit

That noise in the night's not a bedspring—
for alive in the shadows and dust,
a monster stirs down in the basement
and his yawns are loudsqueakers of rust.

The sleepers upstairs in their bedrooms
think it's the furnace that roared;
they don't understand it's Hoodiddit,
who's hungry and cranky and bored.

At midnight he opens the clothes chest—
it's one of his favourite haunts—
and dresses his curious body
in old clothes that nobody wants.

He clamps on the teeth that were Granny's,
dons the corset that Granddaddy wore,
pirouettes in Mom's pink ballet slippers
and slides through his slime on the floor.

His skin has the texture of porridge
that's boiled far too long on the fire:
it's gluey and runny and lumpy—
a skin only monsters admire.

His breath smells as rotten as spinach
too long in the vegetable drawer,
his eyes have the shine that reminds one
of the gleam on a full cuspidor.

When the last light's turned out in the house,
he creeps up the stairs to explore;
he figures it's time to cause mischief—
by sunrise he's done that—and more.

He loves all those living-room snapshots
of relatives at the seashore;
he breathes down the neck of Aunt Dora—
now she's not alone anymore.

In the little girl's room he eats Dolly's shoe,
and one of a pair is one shoe too few.
Whatever is little girl's Dolly to do—
with two naked feet and only one shoe?

Hoodiddit? Hoodiddit?? Who stole Dolly's shoe!
That's exactly the sort of thing little boys do.
Just wait 'til I find him, I'll break his fat nose
and tie him in knots like Mom's pantyhose!

When the little boy hears his sister's wild shriek,
he slams his door shut with his foot.
No sister of his will scold him today—
and anyhow he didn't do it.

In the little boy's room, his favourite bat
leans in the corner alone,
but the boy's pride and joy seems different now—
someone's chewed on that bat like a bone.

Woof? Where's Woof? Hey Woof! Here Woof!!
That dog's gone and ruined my bat.
No, wait! Woof's too dumb—that mutt's got no brain—
it's not him, it's that fleabitten cat!

Soon under the table the dog and cat sit,
nose to nose, not moving a hair;
it was almost as if they liked it like that,
and were quite happy spending time there.

Now the brother and sister scream after the dog
and the dog takes to chasing the cat;
Hoodiddit's all smiles, for in Grandfather's room
he's sunk into something much better than bat.

It is Granddaddy's whisky snitched right from the place
where he'd hidden it just for himself.
You stealing my whisky, Grandmother dear?
Was this bottle not full on that shelf?

Now Granddaddy, dearest, you losing your mind?
Next thing you'll accuse me of drink!
It sure wasn't me, you know that's the truth.
Your son's the one did it, that's what I think!

My son's not a thief! And whatever's gone wrong,
I'm sure that my boy's not to blame.
Look! your perfume's dripped all though my drawers—
I haven't a shirt to my name.

Granddaddy stomped out, he looked red indeed.
From now on I'll sleep on the couch!
That's fine, shouted Granny, I'll have peace and quiet—
my bedroom's no place for a grouch!

At the end of the hall, Dad yelled Hoodiddit?
Who soaked my silk tie in ice cream?
And Mom in the mirror was all in a dither:
Hey, who made my face cream turn green?

Hoodiddit felt happy, he grinned ear to ear
(well, he would've, if he'd had a pair);
now that he'd started the ruckus,
he slipped away down to his lair.

He'd sleep for a week, or a year if he could,
for he dearly likes getting his rest;
but the moment he senses defenses are down,
he arrives like an unwanted guest.

There's a hair in your soup. A stone in your shoe.
A piece of the ceiling drops out of the blue.
What happened? Who did it? You know now, don't you?
It's Hoodiddit who did it, that's who!

At the Library

I'd grabbed The Dictionary to look
something up and out popped
a grasshopper. A dead grasshopper,

perfectly preserved but for a slight
tilt of the head, such as one might exhibit oneself
were one browsing through the *M*s only to come across

a smear of desiccated bug goo scumbling the page; and one
maverick eyeball pressed into the shape of an asterisk
right next to the word 'manifest'—which, says The Dictionary,

means: *plainly apparent to sight or understanding; to reveal;*
to prove. Also: an itemized account of a ship's cargo; the roster
of passengers for an airplane flight; a detailed list of

the cars of a train; and, last: *a fast freight train.*
The sum of such a list may say something
about the development of human consciousness

historico-linguistically speaking, as *all* of these definitions
derive directly from the one Latin word manifestus, meaning,
literally, 'struck by the hand', which is what appears

to have happened to that grasshopper. Perhaps he'd been stuck
on some word on that page in the space between
'Mancunian', that is, *a native of Manchester, England,* and

'maniple', an ecclesiastical word meaning
a band worn on the left arm as a eucharistic vestment;
'Maniple' is also, of course, a non-ecclesiastical word

describing a subdivision of a Roman Legion containing either 60
or 120 men. Such a discrepancy of number would certainly have given the
grasshopper pause: and 'Mancunian' defies all English logic, even if

its etymological provenance is the Medieval Latin,
that most sensible of tongues. True, his investigations
would scarcely have been in the league of inquiry

that deals with the Nature of Good and Evil, say; or whether
God is 'that than which nothing greater can be thought.'
Neither would he have known that a bunch of Roman maniples

were once stationed in Mancunium; that *Mancunium*
became Manchester; and that Manchester was home to a cluster of priests
with armbands. Still, how to distinguish one maniple from another

would have taken that insect-brain well into the night. Sad to relate,
but when whatever Hand of Fate struck that starcrossed head,
that bug'd've found himself transported, teleologically speaking,

a country mile beyond any ability to be inquisitive—or astonished,
or anything! The Librarian, turning the lights off and clearing the desks,
would have shut the book up, and squished it back up on its shelf—

unwittingly contributing evidentiary proof that 'manifest'
was indeed that particular orthopteroid's destiny,
closing in upon him as it did, like the *fast freight train* it is.

On Beheading

It will soothe some to know that death comes almost instantaneously.
And that the head itself falls into a nest of clean straw
down between the knees of an orange jumpsuit,
and doesn't wonder at the sudden footwear

of the executioner, the thick sole
with its frayed fringe of thread keeping the welt
barely connected to the vamp, the metal eyelets
through which the laces run like licorice

crisscrossing neatly up to a long, loose bow
hanging limply down from the crown of the tongue
across the trouser-polished ankle of the boot.
It can't take more than a second or two

for the litres of blood to burst from the severed neck
and evacuate the skull, an instant really—what was it
the good French doctor said: the slice of the guillotine
would feel like a cool breeze, a whisper of the wind.

Painless, really, and requiring less skill than, say, some legendary
scimitar-wielder might exhibit in the village square,
swishing his razor-thin blade through the throat of a standing man,
such that the head would remain aligned, at rest on the dead man's neck.

Molivos

One wave washboarding down
through the black pebbles of Molivos beach,
sheared from a skiff at the arrowhead

of its shining half-mile wake. The craft is working
through water the texture of sanded glass. And me,
I've climbed halfway up the hill with Ray Liotta.

We pause to survey the village's
'rosy-fingered dawn' creep up from the sea,
creep up through the streets to the Castle

which now crowns Molivos with verdigris,
with amber and rubies, with sapphires and eye-aching gold.
A swallow spitfires by on balsa wings

for a beakful of bugs. Bucolic-enough a scene,
but for the strangled gargling of crows
shouldering each other for a spot on the rim

of the smokestack of The Olive Press Hotel.
A boy on a motorbike cranks his engine
and the whole picture-postcard

comes in jigsaw pieces to life. 'Sing!' yells Ray Liotta,
but I can't find the right key among the cockcrows, the dogs'
one-syllable soliloquies, the dialogue of one wretched donkey

rending anguish out of stone. Two mourning doves
on a telephone pole blow their own doleful
vox humana through an oboe, a threnody

in Morse code, *who-who-who* in mezzo-soprano,
tails dipping up-and-down under an invisible
foot-pedal pumping each note out—*who-who-who*,

as two Turkish warplanes howl past the Castle,
keeping the Greeks on their secular toes.
So much for the gauzy subtlety of dawn in the Aegean.

The cats have started, or babies—hard to tell which.
One last bat scribbles by, black bees big as hummingbirds
scout flowers in the diesel thrum of trucks, of trawlers

putt-putting out to sea. A thousand errands to be run
in this maze of brave new worlds. *'Sing, Goddammit!'*
But I can't remember the words as the neighbours

sweep their dust into other neighbours' yards and the lame
lottery-seller clears his throat of at least one of his lungs
with a wet splat of spit, rummaging in his tobacco pouch

for a fresh smoke. And here we are—Commander Ray
and General Me—looking down from the top of the world
at the ignorant army of waves marching pretty much in lockstep

over the deeps where octopodes tussle
with equally meaty fish, and sea-lice make do the best they can
in the maw of the Mediterranean. 'Your dream,' says Ray,

'is packed with emblematic significance—
the way the labyrinthine streets here
are named after various medieval saints,

though the village itself clings temporarily
to cooled volcanic rock, and all the real roads lead
to unknowables lurking beneath the Linnean tables

of the marine biologist or the Latin of the scientists of flora.
Never underestimate the complexity of the universe of whatever
scrounges for the scraps the housewives toss from their doorways,

as even things named are mysterious.' He has
cool blue eyes, does Ray Liotta—and bad skin, it must be said,
but he does drive well. Our rented Suzuki

floats over the cobbles and through the squares effortlessly.
We are studying Molivos in much the same way
you go to see Hamlet brooding on the ramparts

or squatting at the edge of Yorick's grave,
and come home thinking you've 'seen Shakespeare'.
In a manner of speaking, of course, you have.

Ray may not mince words (as plainspoken as he is),
but his notions of how the world works are richer
than the wines of Samos, as layered as the mincemeat

and aubergine of Molivolean moussaka. For example:
the simple stone façade of the Alpha Inn may seem impervious
to Time and earthquake, but it is easily invaded

by the concerns of smirking police and wailing wives,
as in winter the Inn is turned, according to
The Rough Guide to Greece, into the local brothel.

Even now, in the light of a summer's day, we know the village
falls apart after midnight into fragments of dreams
such as this one, as down at the Alpha Inn

a woman sings inconsolably for lost love
and other misfortune (depending on the length
of the set), which has the desired effect of my wanting

to go down there and offer comfort. But then she'd
stop her melodying and all of Molivos would awaken unnerved
that their nocturnal lullaby had ceased to marry

the velvet breezes of their sunless sea
to the bright winds of productive enterprise at daybreak.
Ray's proprioceptive take on this: 'Abyssinia

may well have become Ethiopia, but there's no good reason
you shouldn't visit both countries: the aboriginals still
hold sway in certain facets of the current national imagination;

Jamaican Rastafarians have adapted some of the tenets
of the old doctrines to accommodate life in the New World—
and you gotta love their dreads and baggy hats. Here in Molivos

folks drive scooters as well as donkeys, import bananas,
and seldom squat to shit even though the European
flush toilet uses gallons of precious water.'

Whatever. Ray says the whole town is the self
one needs to rise above to see properly—though, really,
what you see from the Castle is Turkey. Moreover,

if I dream of brothels, policemen and wailing wives, I am
quite likely in the middle of a moral dilemma in Molivos,
which is, after all, a tourist resort full of women

who sunbathe naked at the 'clothing optional' end of the beach.
But I have lashed myself to the mast of my ballpoint pen
in the moored boat of my rented room and have sailed past

the gates of the Alpha Inn with colours flying
and a notebook full of compensatory poems.
Whatever milk and honeydew I need I will

trot down to the shops to get for breakfast, nodding *kalimera*
to the widow Vlakis, whose husband's empty boat
drifted to shore like a dry leaf on the water,

as if to remind the living of the debt they owe to the dead.
Perhaps she'll find comfort in the house of the widow Barbounyi
in Eressos, birthplace of Sappho, who may have helped pave the way

for women better to love one another, as Coleridge himself
might have done with his 'Christabel'. Perhaps had Coleridge
visited Molivos as the Shelleys and the Brownings visited

Bagni di Lucca in Tuscany, he might have composed some decent verse
with Wordsworth driving the twice-five miles of fertile ground,
however distracted he was by laudanum, or by some

man from Porlock, or a madeleine, or one wave
washboarding down on the black pebbles
of a beach in Molivos.

From the Diary of the Sailor's Wife

My sailor mails me hearts, on Post-it notes.
The message scrawled across them: 'I love you.'
They gather on my desk like shipwrecked boats.

I know he thinks I'm his. I'm sure he gloats
amongst his barfly friends: a dismal crew.
He mails me hearts on yellow Post-it notes

but that guarantees him *nada*. Though he dotes
on me, I've several other billets-doux
that gather on my desk like shipwrecked boats.

From dull Land's End, to dreary John O'Groats
they come, the bulk of them with 'Postage Due'.
He mails me hearts on yellow Post-it notes;

the rest send emails, faxes, notes with quotes
of poets, romantic dreck. Sad stuff. What spew!
They gather on my desk like shipwrecked boats.

If truth be told, I'd like to wring their throats.
But then, what would my handsome postman do?
My sailor mails me hearts, on Post-it notes.
They gather on my desk like shipwrecked boats.

Ringmaster

The vinegar smell of piss-yellow straw.
The three teeth left in the old lion's jaw.
The girl on the pony with jiggly bits.
The loaves of manure the elephant shits.

The beer-sticky stains Velcroing seats.
The gossamer meat of the candyfloss treats.
The Chinese contortionist popping her hip.
The cuckolded acrobat losing his grip.

The fluffy French poodles turning their tricks.
The world-weary chimpanzees mining for ticks.
The sad little mouth of Ginger the Clown.
The banker's wife in the next little town.

The suckers in the bleachers clapping like seals.
Everyone knows what the ringmaster feels.

Hang in There

Who amongst us has managed the high-wire
with its gyroscopic soul?
Not I, says Ms Wobbily-Bobbily:
I should have used the pole.

And who has tamed the elephant,
with a whip applied to her bum?
Not I, says Mr Flathead.
Nor I, signs Ms Struck Dumb.

Who's kept the tiger on his perch,
with the arch of an eyebrow
and a lash of pain? I tried, says One-armed Sullivan:
I don't think I'll try again.

Who lived through the crash
of the Krazy Kops car? I did,
and I'm fine, says Benji the Clown:
there's an art to falling down.

The House of Horrors

The House of Horrors is full.
The lineup is longer than Mississippi
where it flows past the old plantations
of cotton and magnolia and murder.

It is longer than the Nile
whose source is the blood of tribes,
whose mouth is salt and Cleopatra,
Cairo and Montgomery, Rommel and Damascus.
The curious have been waiting patiently—

but it is full, there is no room,
and the inadvertent touch has turned to push,
the pushing to punching, the punching to guns
and death. Now the crowd has broken
beyond the circus, beyond the town.
The dead are left on the road

or float down rivers
bumping at the banks of farmers' fields
where buttercups wobble under the sunlight,
under the slightest breeze—and men
and women struggle to get back, to get in—
though there is no room at all, as
the House of Horrors is full.

It is fuller than the bag full of ears,
the ditch full of Jews, the severed heads
full of nothing left at all
after the machetes of the assassins,
or the guns of the king's own Guards,
after all the patient people
who finally made it in.

Concentrate

With dusk come creeping as it does across the provinces,
raccoons descend from their roosts in the trees;
moose big as Ozymandias settle up to their bellies in water

and begin, one huge scoop of tongue at a time,
to drink the lake. But once the wire is set and the rigging steady,
there should be little to make you hesitate but a want of confidence–

unless you were to slip into musing about the various malaises
of domesticity, say, the kids and their adventures in the quotidian
messinesses, the ex-wife, money and whatnot. Sex

is a distraction, you might as well admit that once and for all,
what with its swoons and perfumes, its loosenings and tightenings—
admit that one, then, and then move on. The crossing itself is an act

of balance—that is, of faith in one's ability to remain sure-footed
and perpendicular: nothing more than that, but not a whisper
of anything less. One errant thought about how beautiful the clouds

or how awful the fall and it's game over: the carefully notarized will,
the roof guaranteed for ten years, the car just oiled—all gone
in the middle of whatever wildlife may have engaged your interest

halfway between the swaying buildings or wobbling in the thermals
above a river gathering itself to plunge over a lip of granite
and into the vertigo of space. Whether the mole finds her burrowing

stopped short by material she will never know was once a volcano
is of no consequence, is nothing. Just
concentrate and all will be well, the hawks will settle in their nests

in the stilled rivers of bark, the car spark into life with one turn of the key,
the goal, as ever, that little plot of platform at the end of your leisurely walk,
never the fame bestowed by those upturned faces, nor their dark hope

that they will be the lucky ones to see you fall.

Mephisto, The Human Pincushion

Ah! Good Evening! Apologies for the delay—
a technical glitch—human error, who knows—always
a challenge to get the electricals on stream
in a new 'venue'. Delighted to see so many of you here:
at least we got the cover-charge right!

The lighting's good, don't you think? We especially wanted
this red gel to produce the effect of fire flickering
over my skin—a bit like brandy over a Christmas pudding, no?
Like the dancing mirage of gasoline
before the air itself explodes, the house goes whoosh,
the doctors and cops come running
like dogs to the supperbowl. Two thoughts

to keep in mind before we start: First,
'Happiness has no future.' A kind of seize-the-day
flavour to that, *n'est-ce pas?* Second: 'He was a civilized man
with a penchant for vulgarity.' Pretty good copy
for a tombstone, no? But you're not here
to listen to epitaphs. I know you'll think
that what this maniac is doing is sleight-of-hand,
some bogus smoke-and-mirrors prestidigitation,
I assure you it is not. I am indeed puncturing my arm,
skewering this all-too-human flesh
with this sliver of bamboo, unremarkable, really,
but for the tip I stuffed into a pencil-sharpener.
I remind you that what you paid for was
to see a man put a stick through his arm.
But imagine I'm playing a weird kind
of violin. Imagine hell is the visual metaphor here,
then this back-and-forth slow-bowing of the bamboo
is the Devil's own instrument, a fiddle working
its melancholy temporarily to distract you
from yours. Don't get me wrong: this does hurt; and I do appreciate
your empathy (unless you're a sociopath, in which case
I appreciate your admiration).

I wrote a little verse to accompany this act,
which I would now like to recite for you:

'My childhood was a bramble bush
down at the end of our lane.
I'd carefully pull the brambleberries out
and go back home again.'

Poetry. Never managed to figure out poetry. Managed
to separate the literal from the metaphoric, the visceral
from the imaginative, ended up going into business anyhow
as Mephisto, The Human Pincushion! Go figure. The blood, by the way,
is insensate. Hard to see it in this light, but I can report
that it's an itchy little trickle, quite as irritating
as the wound itself. As if the shimmering liquid
on my arm were not the result of very clever lighting,
but real blood, wet and shining. Chameleonic,
wouldn't you say—how one can abandon oneself
so easily and become someone else, if only
for the length of this performance, right here on this stage?

The Swimmer

They abandoned their houses, the people of Troon,
in 1950, on the 4th of June, in the one hour of sunlight,
that one day a year when the wind went back
to Iceland whence it came.
The water itself was calm as the sea
in some postcard that relatives sent from away.
And there on the street a band of pipes-and-drums
for all the world walking their leisurely, steadily
marching walk, down the long road by the bend of the sea,
down by the seaside and into the square.
Elspeth Morrison met me there.

I was five, she was ten. It didn't matter then
she was plump as a pudding and stuttered when she talked.
I held her hand. We followed the band.

From the beach you could see the municipal pool
with its high-diving tower above the stone wall,
over families on blankets with jam tarts and tea,
over children building castles with seashells and sand,
over Mrs. Finlay's youngest stuffing seaweed down his pants.

Beside my own folks in deckchairs and rugs,
an old man sitting at the edge of the pool,
his teeth and a cake of soap nested neatly on his towel,
his blue wool trunks secured by a length of string
and a knot held fast by collective prayer.
Other elders lounging with their legs in the gelid pool,
that flesh pale as fish chilled in aspic.

Water piped in from the depths of the Irish Sea,
in a line direct from the icy heart of Calvin:
a murky gelatinous bone-numbing slush,
a sludge the consistency
of jellyfish ground through a sieve.

But I would swim
for Elspeth Morrison.

I let her hand go and climbed up the ladder,
past two shivering divingboards
to the platform of the tower.

Beyond my feet my body wobbling,
a small shadow hovering
in that patient block of water
like a shark.

In the distance rose the Ferris wheel
down at the local fair,
and long roads leading
to I didn't know where.
And the sea itself
the simplest map of all—
of how to get to Arran,
to Ireland, to America!

Behind me in line, the old man
clambering stiffly up, one testicle
descended pinkly
from his blue wool trunks.

How still the world stood
beyond that twenty-foot drop,
that three-second measure
of the pleasure of Elspeth Morrison.

'Well, now, young Jimmy: jump
or get off the pot.'

Down on the deck my mother stood,
one hand to her mouth, one hand on the head

of my big-eyed little brother. My father
sucking carefully at the ember in his pipe.

That 4th day of June,
in the one hour of sunlight
at the swimming pool in Troon,
I found the world.

But I jumped
for Elspeth Morrison.

Work

That squat toad, shoulder to
a lily-pad hovering over which
a dragonfly shifts, cruising
the brown slobber of water,
some fish about to glump it down
for lunch, if the toad doesn't get it first.

The canal itself a liquid gloom
in all three dimensions,
its bullion gold sunk deeply
under sunlight that won't stay still,
won't rest, a plastic sandwich box floating by
in freshets of wind, some clots
of soft-fringed, weedy green stuff.

My seven-year-old fishing
for the first time, in the murk, perfect
pike somewhere else, not here. The
mobile rings, his mum asking
everything OK? Better take some
chicken out for supper. Poems somewhere,
and rainbows. Rainbows!

But not much here. Except this one
snapshot of concentration; this distillation
of persistence and—may his father
say it?—the very image
of what is lovely in the world.

My shining little boy.

About the Author

Michael Harris was born in Glasgow, Scotland. He has taught in the English departments of Dawson College and Concordia and McGill Universities in Montreal. He was the founding editor of Signal Editions, the poetry imprint of Véhicule Press. He was twice a winner in the CBC Literary competition and was nominated for the Governor General's Award (poetry) for *Circus* (2010). His most recent book is *Field Notes* (2013), a collection of prose pieces and interviews. He lives in Montreal.